# GROWING

# PERENNIAL FOODS

# GROWING
# PERENNIAL
# FOODS

## A FIELD GUIDE TO RAISING RESILIENT
## HERBS, FRUITS & VEGETABLES

WRITTEN BY ACADIA TUCKER

ILLUSTRATED BY KRISHNA CHAVDA

ISBN: 9780998862354

Library of Congress Catalog Number: 2018944368
Printed in the United States of America
First Printing: 2019
23  22  21  20  19      5  4  3  2  1

Cover design by Krishna Chavda; typography by Katie Craig
Designed and set in type by Mayfly Design

STONE PIER
PRESS
San Francisco, CA

# Contents

Let's Grow Some Good Food . . . . . . . . . . . . . . . . . . . . . . . . . . . . . . . . . . . . . . . ix

It Starts with Good Soil . . . . . . . . . . . . . . . . . . . . . . . . . . . . . . . . . . . . . . . 1

Test Your Soil . . . . . . . . . . . . . . . . . . . . . . . . . . . . . . . . . . . . . . . . . 4

Plan Your Garden . . . . . . . . . . . . . . . . . . . . . . . . . . . . . . . . . . . . . . 7

Build Your Plant Bed . . . . . . . . . . . . . . . . . . . . . . . . . . . . . . . . . . . 11

Choose Your Plants . . . . . . . . . . . . . . . . . . . . . . . . . . . . . . . . . . . . 16

Keep Your Garden Healthy . . . . . . . . . . . . . . . . . . . . . . . . . . . . . . 20

Profiles in Resilience . . . . . . . . . . . . . . . . . . . . . . . . . . . . . . . . . . . 29

**HERBS**

Basil . . . . . . . . . . . . . . . . . . . . . . . . . . . . . . . . . . . . . . . . . . . . . . . . . 33

Chive . . . . . . . . . . . . . . . . . . . . . . . . . . . . . . . . . . . . . . . . . . . . . . . 39

Lavender . . . . . . . . . . . . . . . . . . . . . . . . . . . . . . . . . . . . . . . . . . . . 45

Leaf Fennel . . . . . . . . . . . . . . . . . . . . . . . . . . . . . . . . . . . . . . . . . . 51

Lemon Balm . . . . . . . . . . . . . . . . . . . . . . . . . . . . . . . . . . . . . . . . . 57

Mint . . . . . . . . . . . . . . . . . . . . . . . . . . . . . . . . . . . . . . . . . . . . . . . . 63

Oregano . . . . . . . . . . . . . . . . . . . . . . . . . . . . . . . . . . . . . . . . . . . . 67

Parsley . . . . . . . . . . . . . . . . . . . . . . . . . . . . . . . . . . . . . . . . . . . . . 73

Rosemary . . . . . . . . . . . . . . . . . . . . . . . . . . . . . . . . . . . . . . . . . . . 79

Sage . . . . . . . . . . . . . . . . . . . . . . . . . . . . . . . . . . . . . . . . . . . . . . . 83

Sorrel . . . . . . . . . . . . . . . . . . . . . . . . . . . . . . . . . . . . . . . . . . . . . . 89

Thyme . . . . . . . . . . . . . . . . . . . . . . . . . . . . . . . . . . . . . . . . . . . . . . 93

## FRUITS

Blackberry . . . . . . . . . . . . . . . . . . . . . . . . . . . . . . . . . . . . . . . . . . . . . . . 99

Blueberry . . . . . . . . . . . . . . . . . . . . . . . . . . . . . . . . . . . . . . . . . . . . . . .105

Currant . . . . . . . . . . . . . . . . . . . . . . . . . . . . . . . . . . . . . . . . . . . . . . . . . 111

Goji Berry . . . . . . . . . . . . . . . . . . . . . . . . . . . . . . . . . . . . . . . . . . . . . 117

Grape . . . . . . . . . . . . . . . . . . . . . . . . . . . . . . . . . . . . . . . . . . . . . . . . . 123

Huckleberry . . . . . . . . . . . . . . . . . . . . . . . . . . . . . . . . . . . . . . . . . . . . 129

Raspberry . . . . . . . . . . . . . . . . . . . . . . . . . . . . . . . . . . . . . . . . . . . . . 135

Strawberry . . . . . . . . . . . . . . . . . . . . . . . . . . . . . . . . . . . . . . . . . . . . 141

## VEGETABLES

Artichoke . . . . . . . . . . . . . . . . . . . . . . . . . . . . . . . . . . . . . . . . . . . . . . .149

Asparagus . . . . . . . . . . . . . . . . . . . . . . . . . . . . . . . . . . . . . . . . . . . . . . 155

Beans . . . . . . . . . . . . . . . . . . . . . . . . . . . . . . . . . . . . . . . . . . . . . . . . . 161

Broccoli . . . . . . . . . . . . . . . . . . . . . . . . . . . . . . . . . . . . . . . . . . . . . . . 167

Garlic . . . . . . . . . . . . . . . . . . . . . . . . . . . . . . . . . . . . . . . . . . . . . . . . 173

Pepper . . . . . . . . . . . . . . . . . . . . . . . . . . . . . . . . . . . . . . . . . . . . . . . 179

Radicchio . . . . . . . . . . . . . . . . . . . . . . . . . . . . . . . . . . . . . . . . . . . . . 185

Rhubarb . . . . . . . . . . . . . . . . . . . . . . . . . . . . . . . . . . . . . . . . . . . . . . 191

Spinach . . . . . . . . . . . . . . . . . . . . . . . . . . . . . . . . . . . . . . . . . . . . . . . 197

Sunchoke . . . . . . . . . . . . . . . . . . . . . . . . . . . . . . . . . . . . . . . . . . . . . 203

Sweet Potato . . . . . . . . . . . . . . . . . . . . . . . . . . . . . . . . . . . . . . . . . . . 209

Tomato . . . . . . . . . . . . . . . . . . . . . . . . . . . . . . . . . . . . . . . . . . . . . . . 215

Walking Onion . . . . . . . . . . . . . . . . . . . . . . . . . . . . . . . . . . . . . . . . . . 223

Watercress . . . . . . . . . . . . . . . . . . . . . . . . . . . . . . . . . . . . . . . . . . . . . 229

## RECIPES

**Breakfast**

Currant Yogurt Parfait . . . . . . . . . . . . . . . . . . . . . . . . . . . . . . . . . . . . . . . . . . 115

Goji Berry Granola . . . . . . . . . . . . . . . . . . . . . . . . . . . . . . . . . . . . . . . . . . . . . 121

My Mom's Blueberry Cornmeal Pancakes . . . . . . . . . . . . . . . . . . . . . . . 110

**Dishes**

Balsamic and Honey Roasted Asparagus . . . . . . . . . . . . . . . . . . . . . . . . . 160

Basil Sunflower Seed Pesto . . . . . . . . . . . . . . . . . . . . . . . . . . . . . . . . . . . . . 38

Bean Ragout . . . . . . . . . . . . . . . . . . . . . . . . . . . . . . . . . . . . . . . . . . . . . . . . . 165

Butternut Squash and Sage Risotto . . . . . . . . . . . . . . . . . . . . . . . . . . . . . 87

Cabbage and Fennel Coleslaw . . . . . . . . . . . . . . . . . . . . . . . . . . . . . . . . . 56

Chive and Parsley Hummus . . . . . . . . . . . . . . . . . . . . . . . . . . . . . . . . . . . 43

Couscous Salad with Parsley, Veggies, and Kalamata Olives . . . . . . . . . . 77

Grilled Marinated Artichoke . . . . . . . . . . . . . . . . . . . . . . . . . . . . . . . . . . . 154

Fried Walking Onions . . . . . . . . . . . . . . . . . . . . . . . . . . . . . . . . . . . . . . . . 227

Pasta with Perennial Spinach . . . . . . . . . . . . . . . . . . . . . . . . . . . . . . . . . . 207

Radicchio Salad with Oregano and Orange Vinaigrette . . . . . . . . . . . . . 189

Roasted Sunchokes . . . . . . . . . . . . . . . . . . . . . . . . . . . . . . . . . . . . . . . . . 201

Roasted Tomato Soup . . . . . . . . . . . . . . . . . . . . . . . . . . . . . . . . . . . . . . . 221

Sautéed Mushrooms with Thyme . . . . . . . . . . . . . . . . . . . . . . . . . . . . . . 96

Savory Broccoli Galette . . . . . . . . . . . . . . . . . . . . . . . . . . . . . . . . . . . . . . 172

Sorrel, Spinach, and Lentil Salad . . . . . . . . . . . . . . . . . . . . . . . . . . . . . . . 92

Stuffed Bell Peppers with Tahini Yogurt Dressing . . . . . . . . . . . . . . . . . . 183

Thick-Cut Sweet Potato Fries . . . . . . . . . . . . . . . . . . . . . . . . . . . . . . . . . 213

Tomato Sauce with Oregano . . . . . . . . . . . . . . . . . . . . . . . . . . . . . . . . . . 71

Watercress Salad with Avocado, Cucumber, and Red Onion . . . . . . . . 233

**Dessert**

Baked Peaches and Rosemary . . . . . . . . . . . . . . . . . . . . . . . . . . . . . . . . 82

Raspberry Crisp . . . . . . . . . . . . . . . . . . . . . . . . . . . . . . . . . . . . . . . . . 139

Rhubarb and Apple Pie . . . . . . . . . . . . . . . . . . . . . . . . . . . . . . . . . . 196

**Jams, spreads, and condiments**

Grape and Ginger Chutney . . . . . . . . . . . . . . . . . . . . . . . . . . . . . . . 127

Huckleberry and Lime Jam . . . . . . . . . . . . . . . . . . . . . . . . . . . . . . . 133

Roasted Garlic Spread . . . . . . . . . . . . . . . . . . . . . . . . . . . . . . . . . . . 178

Strawberry Basil Jam . . . . . . . . . . . . . . . . . . . . . . . . . . . . . . . . . . . . 145

**Drinks**

Blackberry Gin Spritz . . . . . . . . . . . . . . . . . . . . . . . . . . . . . . . . . . . 104

Fresh Mint Tea . . . . . . . . . . . . . . . . . . . . . . . . . . . . . . . . . . . . . . . . . 66

Lavender Lemonade . . . . . . . . . . . . . . . . . . . . . . . . . . . . . . . . . . . . 49

**Remedies**

Lemon Balm and Ginger Cough Syrup . . . . . . . . . . . . . . . . . . . . . . .61


Frequently Asked Questions . . . . . . . . . . . . . . . . . . . . . . . . . . . . . . . 235

I don't have a yard. Can I still grow good food? . . . . . . . . . . . . . . . 235

Where can I find information on frost dates? . . . . . . . . . . . . . . . . . 237

How do I make my own compost? . . . . . . . . . . . . . . . . . . . . . . . . . 238

How do I shop for compost? . . . . . . . . . . . . . . . . . . . . . . . . . . . . . . 241

What can I use for mulch? . . . . . . . . . . . . . . . . . . . . . . . . . . . . . . . 242

When and how do I fertilize my plants? . . . . . . . . . . . . . . . . . . . . . 243

What do the three numbers on store-bought fertilizer mean? . . . . . . . . 244

How do I fight weeds without using herbicides? . . . . . . . . . . . . . . . 245

What organic pest solutions can I use? . . . . . . . . . . . . . . . . . . . . . . 247

How do I grow tomatoes and peppers year round? . . . . . . . . . . . . . .251

What's the best way to move a plant from a pot into the ground? . . . . . 252

Glossary . . . . . . . . . . . . . . . . . . . . . . . . . . . . . . . . . . . . . . . . . . . . . . 255

# Let's Grow Some Good Food

**It's 6:30 a.m. and the sun has been up for a little less than an hour.** I roll out of bed and quickly guzzle a cup of coffee. Then I slip on my moss-green muck boots, tattered from many battles with blackberry brambles, and take the well-worn path through the woods to the farm.

Every morning I open a greenhouse filled with beds of peppers, tomatoes, and eggplants. I want to do this before the temperature inside the greenhouse hits 85 degrees and the plants become stressed and thirsty. This morning, when I roll up the plastic sides of the greenhouse, I feel a wave of intense heat escape into the cool air. I check the thermometer inside—90 degrees—and remind myself to wake up earlier tomorrow.

Fortunately, the leaves haven't started to wilt. I breathe a sigh of relief and move on to my morning routine. I start in the back field where a patch of garlic rustles in the soft breeze. I pull weeds and check plants for the dreaded bean beetle. Then I scan the hedgerows of raspberries and currants for the succulent ripe fruits. After admiring the straight rows of potatoes, kale, and beets resting on a bed of straw, I turn on the irrigation system. Now it's time to head to the apple orchard where I'll watch the wildflowers vibrate as hungry bees hunt for nectar. Over at the compost pile, I plunge my hand into the heap to feel its heat.

I love to grow food, plain and simple, and can't imagine doing anything else. When I started farming in Washington at age 21, I focused on practical concerns: finding some land to lease, figuring out which crops to grow, and drumming up enough customers to buy my food. What I didn't give much thought to was climate change. However, after just a few years working this highly weather-dependent job,

I noticed longer frost-free seasons, more intense storms, and more frequent droughts.

Alarmed, I went back to school to study soil management and how it can be a meaningful buffer against weather extremes. When I returned to farming, I started covering my fields every spring with a generous layer of compost. Then I'd lay down another protective layer, this time of straw or wood chips, to keep the compost from washing away and prevent new weeds from sprouting.

Feeding my farm this rich organic material quickly converted the light brown, sandy soil into a dark brown, fluffy bed for my plants. Water sank in instead of pooling on the surface. My plants weathered the heavy rains and occasional droughts of the Pacific Northwest. When I moved back east, I saw how these same methods helped my crops thrive despite New England's harsh winter storms. Eventually, I started to think of myself as a "regenerative farmer."

Regenerative farming is often described as an effort to mimic how nature grows food. Think of a forest that has sustained wild berries, watercress, cherry trees, and other long-lasting perennials for centuries. How does this happen? Leaves and other organic material fall to the ground, protecting the soil from erosion. Insects, fungi, bacteria, and other critters thrive in undisturbed soil and incorporate the fallen material into the ground through their daily activities. This cycle builds a fluffy layer of topsoil packed with nutrients, which supports more plant growth. It's a process that replenishes ecosystems the world over, from forests to fields of wild grains and grasses.

Farmers who take their cue from this process minimize tilling, allowing the healthy microorganisms and bugs that enrich the soil to go about their lives undisturbed. These farmers cover their fields in truckloads of compost. And they plant nutrient-rich cover crops, like Red Clover and Buckwheat. They don't violently break up the soil's texture through plowing. They don't use a lot of chemicals. Their reward? Nutrient-rich topsoil, better water retention, and heartier plants— plus savings on fertilizer, water, and pesticides.

These cost savings help explain why regenerative farming is springing up all over, even in soybean country where industrial farming has long been seen as the most efficient. Some farmers are also motivated by another by-product of organically enriched soil: it draws excess carbon out of the air and stores it underground. This ability to capture greenhouse gases is why many experts believe regenerative agriculture, also known as carbon farming, could play an important role in fighting climate change.

Plants are the ultimate and, dare I say, cheapest way to suck excess carbon dioxide out of the air. Almost all atmospheric carbon passes through plants during photosynthesis, the process that turns carbon, sunlight, and water into sugars and carbohydrates. Plant roots release carbon-rich sugars, which feed organisms in the soil. In exchange, these critters make nutrients in the soil available to the plant. As

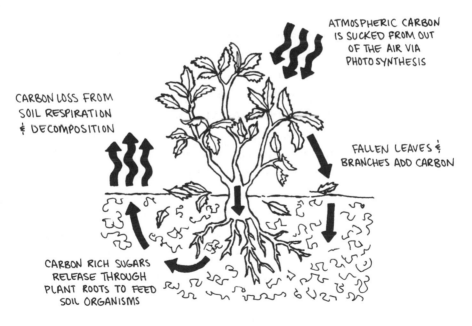

ATMOSPHERIC CARBON IS SUCKED FROM OUT OF THE AIR VIA PHOTOSYNTHESIS

CARBON LOSS FROM SOIL RESPIRATION & DECOMPOSITION

FALLEN LEAVES & BRANCHES ADD CARBON

CARBON RICH SUGARS RELEASE THROUGH PLANT ROOTS TO FEED SOIL ORGANISMS

### SOIL ORGANIC CARBON POOL

*The soil holds twice as much carbon as the atmosphere. Most of the carbon stored underground comes from plants through photosynthesis. As plants flourish, they produce carbon-rich sugars and carbohydrates that travel to the roots and trap carbon below our feet.*

plants die back each winter, they drop leaves and branches and even the roots die off.

Over time this debris decomposes, adding even more nutrients and carbon to the soil. There's evidence to suggest that when living soil organisms die they end up forming even more organic matter than plant residue. The alliance between plants and soil organisms helps lock carbon in topsoil, producing the dark organic matter every gardener lusts for and turning the very ground we stand on into a giant carbon sponge.

Increasing the carbon stored in soil helps to maximize photosynthesis so plants can draw down even more carbon dioxide and trap it underground. Moreover, soil rich in carbon feeds mycorrhizae, a vast network of fungi that releases glomalin. Glomalin is a sticky, gum-like substance that binds together particles of sand, silt, and clay, creating a soil structure that locks in moisture and holds on to nutrients. Plants raised in favorable conditions like this, with easy access to moisture and nutrients, grow sturdier and more resilient. This positive cycle is how nature works when we don't interfere.

Farming in a way that promotes healthy soil is the opposite of how most food is grown. Heavy use of synthetic fertilizers, growing just one crop over large areas, exposing the soil to erosion from wind and water, and tilling are all mainstays of conventional farming, and reduce the amount of carbon in our soil. In 2011, farms emitted six billion tons of greenhouse gases. That's about 13 percent of all greenhouse emissions worldwide, according to the World Resources Institute.

We can turn this around. By adopting regenerative practices, farms could remove carbon dioxide from the atmosphere at a rate of about one ton of carbon dioxide for every acre, according to data reviewed by soil expert Eric Toensmeier. The potential benefits are enormous, as spelled out in a 2014 study from The Rodale Institute. Citing data from farming systems and pasture trials, it concludes that we could sequester more than 100 percent of annual $CO_2$ emissions worldwide if we start growing food this way. The authors write: "Soil carbon sequestration through regenerative agriculture is a known, proven, technical remedy to climate change: it gives humanity the necessary time to decarbonize." Experts agree more study is needed but there's no question that even a small increase in soil carbon can improve crop resilience, reduce chemical use, conserve water on a large scale, and draw down carbon.

The fact that carbon farming could make a difference is both exciting and frustrating. We are, after all, dealing with an agricultural system that does not prioritize health, environmental, or climate concerns. But farmers aren't the only ones who can opt for a regenerative approach. Many of us have our own patches of soil we can tend to—in yards, community gardens, even pots.

I started my own garden after moving from Washington State to New Hampshire to grow hops for local breweries. When I moved, I left behind a farm where we'd grown 200 different food crops. In New England, I so badly missed having fresh fruits, vegetables, and herbs within easy reach that I started my garden almost immediately.

While fewer and fewer people are farmers by profession, many Americans are growing food. In fact, 35 percent of us, or 42 million households, report growing some of our own food, according to the National Gardening Association of America. Just imagine what could happen if more of us took up regenerative gardening. Not only would we have ready access to nutritious, local food. We could help heal the planet.

I developed this book with the beginner in mind. It's for gardeners who want more resilient plants that can withstand extreme weather. It's for people who want to do something about climate change. It's for those who've never grown any food before and want to get started *now*.

The first part of the book describes how to grow food regeneratively. I spend most of it on how to care for your soil—prepping, testing, and nourishing it. Regenerative gardening is unique in how much emphasis it puts on soil health. Indeed, this is why regenerative gardening takes less work than conventional gardening. Your garden simply won't need as much water, pest management, or other caretaking.

The bulk of the book is dedicated to profiles of perennials, a natural choice for regenerative gardeners. These sturdy, long-lived plants are anchored by extensive root systems that help them find water and nutrients deep in the soil. Deep roots also give these plants staying power when they're buffeted by heavy winds, rains, and snow. In addition, having the same plants in the same place for years makes it easier for all the soil-enriching organisms—the bacteria, fungi, and bugs—to gather and multiply.

My favorite time of year is growing season and I end every day with a stroll through my garden. I watch the sunchokes lining the cedar fence track the last bit of sunshine. I look over my tomatoes once more before rolling down the greenhouse walls and tucking them in for the night. I grab a fistful of basil on my way back to the house. And I luxuriate in knowing I'll see these plants again next year.

Weather, soil type, and any number of other variables can make gardening complicated. I've done what I can to keep it simple. I want to make regenerative gardening easy because cultivating even a little bit of carbon-rich soil can make a big difference. Eric Toensmeier estimates that his own tiny carbon-rich backyard garden, about a tenth of an acre, can offset the carbon emissions of one American adult per year. For me, that says one thing: let's grow some good food. It's time.

—*Acadia Tucker*
*Portsmouth, New Hampshire*

# IT STARTS WITH GOOD SOIL

**My first experience harvesting food began with plump, juicy** blueberries during childhood summers in Maine. Washington County is known for its sandy plains of glacially formed barrens on which blueberries love to spread. As a girl, I spent hours hunched over the bushes, raking them clean of ripe berries and taking breaks only to fight off horse flies and mosquitoes. I remember at least one moment when I continued filling my bucket in spite of the itchy welts rising on my arms and legs because of the blueberry pancakes my mother had promised. Naturally, as soon as I had my own land, I planted a few blueberry bushes.

My brand-new blueberry bushes turned into an important lesson about gardening. Blueberries thrive in acidic, or low-pH soil, which supports a particular community of bacteria and fungi. These microorganisms readily release minerals like iron, which blueberries need a lot of to thrive. Commercial growers emphasize adjusting your soil's pH before planting anything, but I didn't want to hear it. I wanted to bring a little piece of Maine to my new home in the Pacific Northwest and couldn't wait to get those bushes in the ground. I told myself I could fix any problems later.

My backwards approach to soil prep didn't work. Even after a year, the plants had barely fruited. I tried lowering the pH by piling on pine needles, pine bark, and sawdust. Nothing happened. I tweaked and adjusted my compost some more, willing the fruit to appear. It never did. I could have tried other tactics, including adding rock minerals. But after the fourth year, I realized that my dream of raising healthy blueberry bushes would be more likely to happen if I just started over.

Four years of fresh blueberry pancakes lost, thanks to my failure to acidify the soil *before* planting bushes.

What I learned is that there are no quick fixes or shortcuts to preparing healthy soil for your perennials. But if you start off right, and stick with it, your reward will be a crop of plants that practically take care of themselves. Readying your soil, whether starting fresh or building onto an existing garden, consists of testing it, clearing out weeds, adding plenty of compost and mulch, and—once your plants are in the ground—doing as little as possible to disturb the dirt around them.

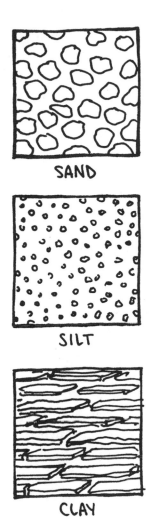

SAND

SILT

CLAY

Not all soil is equal. The three main categories are sand, silt, and clay. Sandy soil is made from large particles that create a lot of space in the soil for water and nutrients to occupy. But it also drains very quickly, washing away the nutrients and leaving your soil dry and infertile. Clay soil is the opposite. It's made of very small, tightly packed particles. The smaller spaces between soil particles make it difficult for water to percolate through, but once it's there, water is slow to drain. Silt soils fall somewhere between sand and clay, and are made of loosely packed, medium-sized particles. This structure allows water and nutrients to soak into the soil and stay there for plants to use. The soil in your garden can be any combination of these three soil types but the most sought-after combination is loam. Loam is 40 percent sand, 40 percent silt, and 20 percent clay. Sandy or clay soil can behave like loam if you give it enough compost.

# TEST YOUR SOIL

**Every once in a while, I grab a handful of moist dirt** from my garden and squeeze it. What I'm looking for is texture. If it crumbles, my soil is too dry and sandy and I'll have to add more compost. If it holds its shape even after some poking, the soil contains too much clay and I'll have to mix in peat, calcium carbonate, lime, or sand to break it up and improve drainage. If my clod holds its shape and falls apart only after I prod it, then I probably have rich, well-drained loam soil, which most perennials love.

Testing the quality of your soil isn't absolutely necessary for carbon gardeners. You can address most major problems through the usual process of weeding, composting, mulching, and preparing your soil for planting. However, the occasional soil test can be a helpful gauge of what's working and whether you need to pile on more compost or other fertilizers or loosen compacted soil, so I've built soil testing into my annual routine and recommend you do, too. Just don't let a soil test hold you back. Starting a garden today is better than not starting one at all.

Most state universities can test your soil inexpensively and give you a detailed profile that includes pH and nutrient levels. Nutrient tests also tell you how much organic matter you have in your soil. You'll want to aim for three to six percent. Knowing what nutrients your soil already contains can help you limit fertilizer use, since well-established perennials don't need much boosting. In fact, by fertilizing them you run the risk of weakening these plants.

While lab tests can be useful, nothing can replace the old-fashioned, immediate gratification of what I call the "earthworm test." If you've got these crawlers, your soil is probably in great shape because

*Healthy soil is filled with organisms that break down organic matter, providing nutrients and aerating the soil. Through their daily activities, organisms large and small help build carbon into the soil. (A) Large animals like moles and other burrowing rodents tunnel through the soil, opening up big pockets that let water soak in deep. (B) Earthworms decompose organic materials, releasing nutrients for plants to use and aerating the soil as they travel. (C) The rhizosphere, or the area around plant roots, is filled with small soil organisms like mites, nematodes, mycelium, and microbes that aid in decomposition, helping to keep carbon underground.*

they signal the presence of millions of other smaller organisms. If you don't have earthworms, you've got work to do. These hardworking critters convert minerals and organic matter into nutrients for plants. They also aerate the soil so plant roots can grow freely. Plus, they tickle the palm of your hand if you hold them gently.

I do my earthworm test every spring after the soil has warmed up to at least 55 degrees. This ensures the worms are awake and moving around after their winter slumber. I rely on a soil thermometer. If you don't have one, wait until you've had a few weeks of warm weather before digging up your worms.

To start, dig a hole roughly one foot wide and one foot deep. Shovel the dirt onto a piece of cardboard, newspaper, or tarp. Gently sift through the dirt, carefully pulling aside any earthworms you find. I look for at least 10 earthworms in my sample. If I've got that many in a square foot of soil, I know it's well aerated and getting the nutrients it needs. After I'm done counting, I usually toss the worms into my compost bin so they can help break down food scraps into more plant nutrients.

If your earthworm count comes up short, you may have dry, compacted soil that's light on organic matter. Try mixing two inches of compost into the first four inches of your soil. Wait a few months before running another earthworm test. If they're still scarce, add more compost and repeat.

# PLAN YOUR GARDEN

**When I farmed in the Pacific Northwest,** it was my first experience growing food on a large scale. I worked the land on a tiny peninsula that jutted into the Strait of Georgia, right on the U.S.-Canadian border. My farm was in Washington State, but the mainland was Canadian.

I'd been prepared for Washington's famously wet winters. But the drenchings were so frequent that I grew to resent the pewter gray skies, even if the rains did bring a flush of brilliant green growth as soon as the soil warmed. All that moisture stored in the soil meant I didn't have to water the crops until June. Since there was no well on the property and regulations forbade digging any future wells, I had to rely on expensive municipal water imported from Canada. For this reason, rain was truly my best friend—except when it wasn't. Our farm was hit by winter storms that could dump five inches of rain or more, all at once, a phenomenon that's been plaguing growers more frequently since our warming air can hold more moisture.

The heavy rains were bad. But I really didn't expect the scorching hot summers, which left plants gasping for moisture. One year we had no measurable rain for 52 straight days. Our northerly location also meant we had more than 15 hours of sunlight a day in midsummer. Try finding plants that can survive the short, cool days of spring *and* thrive in all that summer sun!

One day in late August, I was walking past a sorry-looking lineup of shriveling plants and suddenly saw one of the problems: I'd stuck moisture-loving plants in dry, sandy soil. Not too far off to the left, I spotted another problem: there was a tired-looking shade-loving plant bearing the brunt of the full mid-afternoon sun. The sight of these unhappy plants made me realize I needed to draw a planting site map.

Over the next few days, I really studied my land. I watched where the sun fell at different times of the day. I probed the soil for moisture. I took note of the soggy dips and well-drained mounds. I dug my trowel in deep to see where the soil was sandy or dense, dry or moist. I observed the prevailing winds to determine where my tender herbs could find shelter. Then I drew my map.

Once I'd sketched in the shady zones, the well-drained areas, and the sandy spots, I planned out where to transfer existing plants and add new ones. I planted red currants on the edge of the field. The tall plants could help protect my top-heavy broccoli from being blown over, and their shade help keep the soil moist. I moved drought-tolerant goji berries to the front of the farm, which had lots of dry, gravelly soil. I transferred my water-loving strawberries to small dips in the ground near the greenhouse because that area stayed moist throughout the summer.

I built new trellises for runner beans next to sensitive crops like lettuce and spinach so they'd get the shade they need. I built up mounds of soil with compost to improve drainage for my artichokes and rhubarb so they'd have an easier time surviving the wet winter. And I tore out my more demanding plants like sweet potatoes, which don't do well in regions that swing between flooding and drought, and replaced them with almost-anything-goes garlic.

Next I visited garden supply stores for more ideas for plants because I wanted food that thrives locally. Soon I had raspberry bushes that pumped out juicy fruit, even when I forgot to water them.

## Draw your site map

It's not hard to draft a site map. A pencil and a sheet of graph paper are all you need. Make each block represent 10 feet by 10 feet. You can also print out a Google Earth view of your property and use that as a starting point. Here's what you'll want to do:

- Mark where your site gets full sun throughout the day.
- Pencil in the areas with patches of afternoon shade or full shade.
- Note where your soil is mostly clay, mostly sand, or a mix of both.
- Figure out the direction of the prevailing wind in case it makes sense to build a wind break.
- Indicate where the land is hilly and drains well or stays wet.

Once you've laid out your map, place plants where they have the best chance of doing well based on the sun, water, and soil conditions they prefer. See "Perennial Characteristics" (page 18) for guidance on choosing compatible plants.

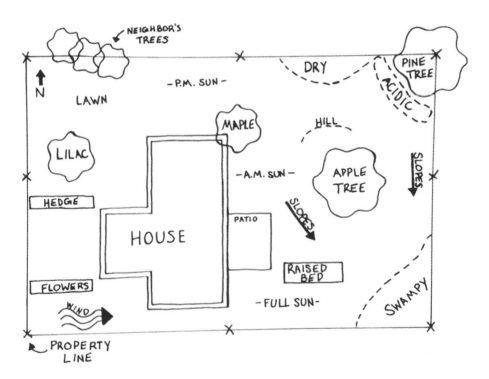

*The first step to planning a successful garden is to know your site so you can place plants where they're most likely to thrive.*

I know matching a plant to its environment sounds like common sense, but it wasn't obvious to me what a difference it can make until I saw it for myself. Now I draw a map for every garden I grow. Not only are my plants happier and less demanding, but I no longer fret in the middle of the night when torrential rains beat down or drought hits. I have more mental space to enjoy myself and my garden.

# BUILD YOUR PLANT BED

**The hardest practice for me to adopt on my way to becoming a** regenerative grower was low-till farming. Running a big metal rototiller through dirt is a really efficient way to break up weeds and grass and dig seed furrows. Unfortunately, this machine also breaks apart the soil's natural structure and the living soil community that works so hard to nourish plants. So I eventually gave up the rototiller.

Instead, I've learned to grow my food on raised beds. With raised beds, you can leave soil organisms alone so they can go about their lives, breaking down organic matter, recycling nutrients, and aerating the soil. The structure they give the soil makes for good drainage, wicking away excess water in the winter and spring so roots don't rot while keeping soil moist but not soggy in the summer. Well-drained soil also warms up faster in the spring because any moisture that remains absorbs the sun's heat. This same property helps keep plants warm when nights are nippy.

I don't think tilling can be entirely avoided. It's hard to sow seeds through a mat of grass roots or leftover plant matter without using a potato fork, and it's difficult to uproot weeds without a hoe. Minimal tilling, disturbing only the first few inches of the soil, is realistic, and it actually reduces a new plant's need for fertilizer.

Garden beds can be any size and live anywhere in your garden. You can build on top of existing garden beds or make new ones. Typically, you'll only have to build a bed once. To start, you can head to the hardware store to buy wood, then build a box and fill it with soil. But I prefer skipping the box in favor of layering compost, shredded leaves, and other yard waste directly on the ground. It's less expensive and produces good soil in the process.

**Pick a location.** You'll want to locate your bed in an area that allows you to walk around or next to it. You'll also want to consider the width. Can you easily reach across to tend plants? Stepping on your beds will compact, or squeeze together, soil particles. Without air pockets, it's harder for soil to absorb water and store nutrients. Compacted soil also crowds out all those good organisms you want to invite into your garden.

**Prep your plot.** If you're building beds over turf or weedy areas, you'll have to kill off these plants first, ideally without bringing out the heavy machinery. Sheet mulching, which calls for layering on cardboard, dead leaves, grass clippings, or other organic material, is my favorite approach because it builds good soil while smothering weeds. But it isn't the only way to clear your ground for planting. Here's more about mulching, plus two other reliable ways to start a garden.

1. **Sheet mulch your plot.** You'll need cardboard or newspaper, leaves, grass clippings, compost, and any other organic material you can get your hands on. First, lay moistened cardboard or newspaper over your lawn. If you plan on planting large woody perennials like fruit bushes, cut a hole in the cardboard and plant your bushes through the hole. Then layer on grass, leaves, and compost in thick layers, about two inches each, and repeat until the materials run out. For best results, you'll want to do this at least twice. The thick mat of material not only smothers weeds and but also buries seeds so future weeds are less of a problem. If you planted perennials before sheet mulching, take care to clear any materials from the base of each plant so it has at least a three inch bare ring around it.

   You may be surprised at first by the height of your bed. Give it time. Busy soil organisms will quickly shrink the pile of organic material. For now, finish off your heap with some fresh topsoil or well-aged compost if you want to plant right away. Otherwise, it's fine to just let it sit.

Sheet mulching isn't for everyone. For one thing, it takes time for a pile to break down. I rely on sheet mulching when I'm clearing a large area and there's no rush. If you want to give it a try, I recommend starting in late summer for the next year's planting.

2. **Till, but gently.** Tilling is hard to give up completely because it's such an effective way to tear out grass, especially if you don't have the time—or all that cardboard!—to sheet mulch. But there's mechanical tilling that pulverizes soil structure, and then there's biological tilling. This gentler approach focuses on building healthy soil by using the earthworms, fungi, and bacteria that naturally loosen and aerate the soil. To create a new bed, use a spade, hoe, and potato fork to dig up clumps of sod until the ground is bare. This can take a lot of work, but you'll only have to do it once.

   After clearing out the grass and weeds, you'll need to loosen the soil. Take a shovel and dig a trench along the edge of your new bed, dumping the soil in a wheelbarrow if you have one. Fill the trench by digging a new one right next to the first. As you dig the second trench, toss the soil into the first one. Repeat this process until the entire bed has been trenched and filled. After digging your final trench, fill it with the soil you set aside in the wheelbarrow. Now that all the soil has been loosened, level the bed with a rake, and it's ready to go.

3. **Just add soil.** There's another way to prepare your planting bed: add more soil. First, clear off the grass and weeds using either tilling or sheet mulching, as described above. Then shovel on soil from anywhere in your yard, as long as you've first removed all the weeds. If your yard is too weedy or hard to dig up, or just not all that big, buy a few bags of soil from your local garden center. Make sure any soil you buy is dark brown and clear of debris. I

mention this because poor-quality leftover construction fill is sometimes rebranded as garden soil. Add enough soil so the bed is three to eight inches high. Any higher and you run the risk of having soil wash away during big storms or intense rainfall. Plus, it may dry out more quickly.

**Prime your soil with compost.** Once you've eliminated any weeds and grass and built your bed, it's time to jump-start the growing process by working compost into the top three inches of your soil. Compost is decomposed organic material that can work miracles in

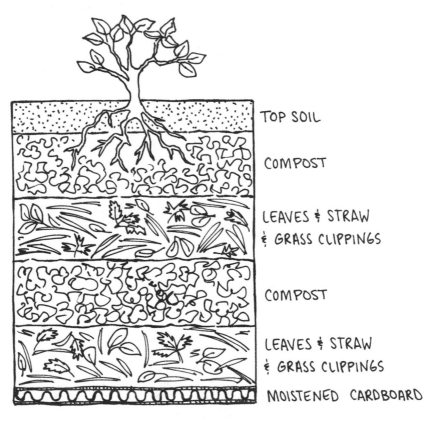

TOP SOIL

COMPOST

LEAVES & STRAW & GRASS CLIPPINGS

COMPOST

LEAVES & STRAW & GRASS CLIPPINGS

MOISTENED CARDBOARD

*Build your garden bed from the ground up, starting with a layer of moistened cardboard followed by alternating layers of straw, leaves, grass clippings, and compost to smother weeds and create nutrient-dense soil for planting.*

a garden. Packed with nitrogen, phosphorus, and other nutrients, it can be made of everything from kitchen scraps to yard waste. One small handful teems with millions of beneficial soil dwellers, from the tiniest decomposer microbes to nutrient-recycling nematodes and, larger still, soil-moving earthworms. All of these eat carbon for energy and, in the process, break down organic matter into plant-available nutrients that help you grow tasty crops. In addition, these creatures give your soil a porous, open structure so water can penetrate, instead of running off, increasing soil erosion and polluting waterways with sediment. *Note:* You won't have to add more compost during the planting process if you've opted to use sheet mulching or good soil from a gardening store. But you'll still want to refresh your beds with compost each spring after your garden is established.

# CHOOSE YOUR PLANTS

**My long winter nights are generally spent poring over every seed** catalog that finds its way into my mailbox. Thinking about the tomatoes, beans, and beets I'll plant in the spring helps me get through the bitterly cold winters here in New Hampshire. And when the weather warms up and my dreams of garden-fresh food turn into a full-blown planting frenzy, I'm grateful for my perennials. Because while I'm planting the tiny seeds I've saved, waiting for that first tender head of lettuce to appear, I already have glorious asparagus spears pushing through the still-chilled soil, begging to be steamed and eaten with butter and lemon.

It wasn't always this way. I've learned over time what thrives on my land and what doesn't. I've learned what I like to eat and what ends up way too often as compost. Too many times I've planted something because it's doing well in a friend's yard or just looks nice, only to realize I don't have any interest in eating it.

So here's my first piece of advice: plant what you actually want to bring into your kitchen. If you love making stir-fry, then plant walking onions, perennial broccoli, and garlic. If you like savory stews, grow sunchokes, sweet potatoes, and oregano. If you're crazy about fresh-baked desserts, fill your garden with rhubarb, blackberries, and strawberries. Food gardens aren't necessarily pretty or neat, and that's okay. You're growing food, not ornamental plants.

In addition to growing food you'll actually eat, you'll want plants that can weather today's climate extremes. This entire book is dedicated to those plants but it's also possible to increase the odds they will be sturdy, pest resistant, and resilient.

**Go for variety.** Natural ecosystems are a mosaic of soil types, plants, and animals, each supporting the growth of the other. Your yard is no different, so plant accordingly. The more diverse your plantings, the better your garden will withstand floods, drought, and big temperature swings.

I've planned my garden so the shrubs and trees in my yard provide summer shade and some protection against winter winds. I included plants of varying heights and with different light requirements, making use of every inch of space. My food ripens at different times, so I almost always have something fresh from the garden to eat. And along with annual favorites like corn and peas, I mix in deep-rooted perennials to feed the soil flora and fauna.

Choosing a variety of plants that produce shade and are constantly flowering puts out the welcome mat for the beneficial bugs that pollinate crops, like honey bees and wasps, or the ones that devour aphids, like lacewings and spiders. Spiders are truly a gardener's friend, by the way. The world's spider population, which weighs in at nearly 25 million tons, eats up to 800 million tons of insects each year!

**Choose locally.** Zero in on plants that thrive in your own backyard and you'll have a head start on a healthy garden. Local plants have already adapted to the soil and climate where you live. When I first moved to New England, my priority was finding plants that could survive our winters and ripen quickly during the short summers. I found most of the answers at a garden supply store, one I still visit to stay current on new arrivals and regional resources.

**Match your plants to your location.** This is the culmination of the work you started with your site map. After testing your soil, studying your site, and capturing what you learned on your map, there's one last step, which is to find the most suitable plants (see "Perennial Characteristics," p. 18). This means choosing shade-loving plants for areas that get little sun, rugged plants for windy zones, and plants that love acidic soils for low pH zones.

# Perennial Characteristics

| | Name | Good Groundcover | Drought-Tolerant | Shade-Tolerant | Good for containers |
|---|---|---|---|---|---|
| **Herbs** | Basil | | | | x |
| | Chives | | x | x | x |
| | Lavender | | x | | x |
| | Leaf Fennel | | | | x |
| | Lemon Balm | x | x | x | x |
| | Mint | x | x | x | x |
| | Oregano | x | x | | x |
| | Parsley | | x | x | x |
| | Rosemary | x | x | | x |
| | Sage | | x | | x |
| | Sorrel | x | | x | x |
| | Thyme | x | x | x | x |
| **Fruits** | Blackberry | | | | |
| | Blueberry | | | x | x |
| | Currant | | | x | x |
| | Gogi Berry | | x | | x |
| | Grape | | x | | |
| | Huckleberry | | x | x | |
| | Raspberry | | | x | |
| | Strawberry | x | | | x |
| **Vegetables** | Artichoke | | | | |
| | Asparagus | | x | | |
| | Beans | | | x | |
| | Broccoli | | | x | x |
| | Garlic | | x | | x |
| | Pepper | | x | | x |
| | Radicchio | | | x | |
| | Rhubarb | | x | x | |
| | Spinach | | | | x |
| | Sunchoke | | | | |
| | Sweet Potato | | | | |
| | Tomato | | x | | x |
| | Walking Onion | | x | x | |
| | Watercress | | | | x |

*Table 1. Knowing a perennial's particular preferences makes it easier to choose the right plants for your plot.*

CHOOSE YOUR PLANTS

| Grows in acidic soil | Good for sandy soil | Good for clay soil | Spring Harvest | Summer Harvest | Fall Harvest |
|---|---|---|---|---|---|
| | | | | X | X |
| | | | X | X | X |
| | X | | | X | |
| | | | X | X | X |
| | X | | | X | X |
| | | | | X | X |
| | X | | | X | X |
| | | | X | X | X |
| | X | | X | X | X |
| | X | | | X | X |
| X | | | X | | X |
| | X | | X | X | X |
| X | X | | | X | |
| X | X | | | X | |
| | | | | X | |
| | X | | | X | |
| | X | | | X | |
| X | X | | | X | |
| X | X | | | X | X |
| | X | | X | X | |
| | X | | X | X | X |
| | X | | X | | |
| | X | | | X | |
| | X | | | X | X |
| | X | | | X | |
| | X | | | X | X |
| | X | X | | X | X |
| | | | X | X | |
| | | | | X | X |
| | X | | | | |
| X | X | | | | X |
| | X | | | X | X |
| X | X | | X | X | X |
| | | | X | X | X |

# KEEP YOUR GARDEN HEALTHY

**Getting your plants in the ground is only the beginning. The next** step is developing a maintenance plan that works for you, and builds greater resilience in your plants with every passing year.

I've learned to greet each spring by clearing out the weeds and laying down an inch or two of compost, followed by a couple of inches of mulch. For really overgrown areas I use damp cardboard as a ground barrier and cover it with mulch. Once I've done all that, and pruned any dead or damaged stems and branches, I give my plants enough water to battle the summer heat and gear up to regularly weed and scan plants for signs of disease or pests.

No growing season is exactly the same, of course, and global warming has introduced even more variables. Drought, a sudden influx of pests, or an increase in extreme storms greatly influences how a garden grows. I also like to experiment with new perennials and ways to bolster my soil ecosystem. But any good maintenance plan is by definition pretty flexible. Build the following elements into your own routine and your regenerative garden will not only grow, but thrive.

## Compost and mulch

Compost and mulch work their magic better when used together. Basically, compost is what you mix into your soil and mulch is what you lay on top of it. It's good practice to apply both to your garden before planting, and replenish these layers every year.

This potent blend helps keep moisture in the ground by increasing the amount of carbon-rich organic matter. Enriched soil holds more water than mere dirt thanks to plenty of space between soil particles, which lets in air and water. Compost is also packed with nutrients plants love. Refreshing the mulch around your plants once or twice a year helps prevent the erosion of this rich topsoil, keep nutrients in the ground, and protect plant roots so they're less likely to dry out or freeze. (To make your own compost and mulch, see pages 238-242.)

## Fertilize, as needed

Perennials are known for being low maintenance. An annual dose of compost and mulch is all the nourishment most will ever need. But there are times even these hardy plants need extra help. A yellowing currant bush might benefit from a nitrogen-rich fertilizer. A sprinkling of lime might be just the thing for tomatoes suffering from blossom end rot. Whatever the case, when it comes to choosing additional fertilizers a gardener has two main options: a fast-acting synthetic fertilizer or a slow-release organic fertilizer.

Synthetic fertilizers are made of soluble salts that plants immediately absorb through their roots. If you've ever used one you know how quickly plants respond to the boost. But making synthetic fertilizers is energy intensive, relying on nonrenewable resources like coal. They're also detrimental to soil health. The salt they leave behind acidifies soils, pushing out beneficial decomposers like earthworms and fungi. For every season you use synthetic fertilizer, you have to add more of it the following year to get the same results.

Organic fertilizers are made from plant and animal materials. Rich in organic matter, they rely on insects, fungi, and bacteria to break them down, slowly releasing nutrients into the soil and building overall fertility. While the slow release of nutrients doesn't have the same kick as a synthetic fertilizer, they stay in the ground longer and don't leach into the surrounding environment as easily. Organic fertilizers also contain the micronutrients plants need, like iron, manganese, and calcium. (For more information on when and how to use organic fertilizers, sec pages 243-244.)

## Water

I have two hard rules when it comes to watering. First, water the soil and not the plants. Keeping moisture off leaves reduces the chance of diseases like mold and mildew. And water on leaves often evaporates before it has a chance to reach the ground. Second, rely on long, deep watering sessions rather than frequent, shallow ones.

A good rule of thumb is to make sure your plants get an inch or two of water a week in total, from rainfall or watering. This lets your soil dry out between sessions, discouraging root disease and promoting deep, strong root growth. With shallow watering, roots are less likely to travel deep into the soil and more likely to be hurt by drought and wind.

## Prune and weed

Regular pruning can stimulate growth in young plants and revitalize established perennials. I prune in spring to remove dead or diseased branches, and in summer to manage a plant's shape and size. No need to prune late in the season. Frost will likely kill any new growth, wasting precious energy a plant could otherwise use to hunker down for the winter. Use sharp shears so you can make a clean cut and avoid stripping the protective bark.

Weeds are a pain because they are seed producing machines. Lambsquarter, for instance, can produce more than 50,000 seeds a year. If your garden is overrun by weeds, clearing your beds can quickly turn into a never ending chore. The trick is to prevent weeds from going to seed in the first place, which means yanking them before they bloom. This makes spring an opportune time to clear weeds.

During the summer I'm usually too busy to worry about unwanted plants so rather than weed, I mulch. Mulch helps keep weed seeds from sprouting. Any plants that do succeed in pushing through the protective layer are usually weak from the effort, making them easy to pull out.

If you're short on time, target perennial weeds like red dock, dandelions, and thistle that settle into a garden and come back stronger and more rooted each year. Keep at it and you'll be rewarded with fewer and fewer weeds every year. (For more tips on battling weeds, see pages 245-246.)

## Aerate the soil

You'll probably want to loosen up the soil in your garden beds every year so it stays porous. In spring, after the soil has dried, bring out your broadfork, a U-shaped tool with heavy metal prongs that can loosen soil up to a foot deep. It's foolproof, requires no fossil fuels, and protects the community of critters beneath your feet.

To use the tool, hold the handles in each hand and step on the bottom of the U, or crossbar, with the metal prongs facing down. Use all your body weight to drive the prongs into the soil and step back, pulling the handles toward your body. This forces the prongs upward through the soil, gently breaking up any compaction and creating deep channels so water can drain into the root zone. I also like to add one heaping wheelbarrow of compost to my beds every spring, enough to cover them with at least an inch of this wonderful stuff.

If you keep this up, you can't help but begin to notice the change in your soil. Sandy soil will hold more nutrients and water. Clay soil will loosen up and drain more freely. Either will behave more like loam. See what happens when you pull up a weed. If the roots are spread out and the soil crumbles away easily, you have pretty good soil. The time to add more compost is when you pull up a plant and see stunted roots that are either naked or have soil clinging stubbornly to them.

# Manage pests and disease

With its lively community of organisms, healthy soil does a pretty good job of fighting common garden pests and diseases naturally. Predatory nematodes attack insects that overwinter in your garden soils while parasitic fungi kill bad bugs by penetrating their tough skin.

Thriving soil also hides your garden from pests. Stressed and nutrient-deficient plants release pheromones, distress calls that draw bugs of all kinds to come and feast on your garden. Plants and bugs evolved together this way so that weak plants fail, making it easier for healthy plants to reproduce and prosper. Still, a garden can fall prey to a bug invasion or disease outbreak no matter how healthy the soil.

To keep pests under control I monitor my garden closely and act quickly to contain the damage when I see a problem. I rely on a combination of mechanical strategies, like hosing down and even picking off bugs, and organic solutions, like spraying leaves with insecticidal soap. I never use herbicides because of the environmental damage they can do, and my crops don't suffer for it.

The best advice I can offer is to give your plants room to breathe. Overcrowded plants are more susceptible to diseases like powdery mildew, and invite pests to feed by giving them a place to hide. (For recommendations on organically certified pest solutions, visit page 247.)

# A seasonal guide to your regenerative garden

| SPRING | |
|---|---|
| **Composting** | Work at least an inch of compost into your soil before sowing any seeds. For seedlings, mix compost into the bottom of your hole before dropping in your plant. Spring is also the perfect time to spread a layer of compost around the base of established plants. |
| **Mulching** | Top your compost with at least one inch of mulch, except for freshly seeded beds. Mulch makes it harder for seeds to germinate. |
| **Planting** | Wait until the ground has thawed and the weather has warmed to plant seeds, cuttings, and seedlings outside. Introduce indoor plants to the outdoors gradually. One week before transplanting, start moving your pots outside for a few hours a day. |
| **Pruning** | Cut out any diseased or storm-damaged branches. |
| **Additional Fertilizing** | To boost your growth beyond what your plants get with compost consider adding a nitrogen-heavy fertilizer, but not too much. Overfertilizing can yield leggy plants that flop over. |
| SUMMER | |
| **Composting** | Give your nutrient-hungry plants, like broccoli, an extra handful of compost around the base. |
| **Planting** | There's still time to plan and plant a garden, if you use seedlings. To protect new plants from heat stress, move them into the ground in the early morning or evening, or on gray days. |
| **Supporting** | Many perennials benefit from some sort of support, whether it be a trellis, stake, or garden twine. By preventing plants from flopping over you'll keep them healthy longer. |
| **Watering** | It's hot outside. Make sure to water your plants all summer long. |

*Knowing what to do and when can be a challenge for beginning gardeners. Follow this seasonal guide and your garden will likely thrive.*

| | |
|---|---|
| **Pruning** | Trim your plants to manage disease and keep them from getting too big. As a general rule, don't whack off more than a third of a plant at a time or you might send it into shock. |
| **Additional fertilizing** | So much energy goes into ripening food that plants can get stressed, which attracts pests. Consider adding bone meal to your perennials once they flower to boost phosphorus levels and make them stronger. |
| **Pest and disease management** | Regularly check your plants for bugs and signs of disease. Try to deal with any problems right away to minimize the risk of spreading. |

**FALL**

| | |
|---|---|
| **Planting** | Plant any new bare root shrubs well before the first frost so they have time to become established before winter sets in. |
| **Composting** | Cover your soil with up to an inch of compost to give healthy organisms a chance to thrive and multiply come spring. |
| **Mulching** | Lay down a protective layer of mulch over the compost to keep it from washing away and protect plant roots from the damage caused by repeated freezing and thawing. |
| **Watering** | Even when the weather cools it's not a bad idea to water your plants weekly. |
| **Pruning** | Don't bother pruning. It only encourages new growth, which will likely die when the cold sets in. |
| **Additional fertilizing** | If you want to improve your odds for a bigger harvest next year, go ahead and sprinkle on a little phosphorus- and potassium-based fertilizer like bone meal and kelp meal. Don't overdo it or the excess will wash away in the winter rain. |

**WINTER**

Protect your plants from the cold by bringing them inside or covering them with a floating row cover. Winter is a time for plants to rest, unless you live in a climate that's warm all year round. If that's the case, keep on growing and harvesting!

# GARDENING TOOLS: A STARTER PACK

*With so many options available, choosing gardening tools can be overwhelming. These are the ones I can't do without.*

BROAD
FORK

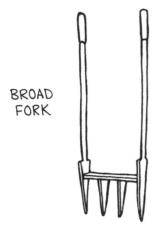

HARVESTING
KNIFE

*I use this to deeply aerate soil without turning it over so soil structure and organisms are preserved.*

*I harvest my food with this serrated, curved knife. It's so sharp it does the job without damaging the rest of the plant.*

LONG
HANDLED
HOE

*The long handle lets me tackle light weeding without breaking my back.*

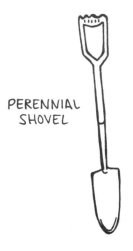

## PERENNIAL SHOVEL

*The narrowness of the blade allows me to plant in tight spaces or established gardens without disturbing the soil too much.*

## POTATO FORK

## WEEDING KNIFE

*I use this tool for almost everything. It's especially handy for mixing in compost and rooting out large weeds.*

*This sturdy knife makes it easier to remove stubborn tap roots and anything else that's hard to dig out, like dock and thistle.*

# PROFILES IN RESILIENCE

**Look into most backyard vegetable gardens and you're likely to** see carrots, lettuce, zucchini, maybe some corn. These are the vegetables most people know and love. I do, too. But since you're reading this, I'm guessing you're open to taking a chance on lesser-known plants. Plants with romantic names like walking onion, goji berry, and Scarlet Runner Bean. Plants that will be with you, year after year, without needing much attention. Plants, well rooted and sturdy, that support the growth of healthy soil ecosystems that conserve water and offset carbon emissions.

The perennials I've chosen to highlight include popular plants, like garlic, peppers, and strawberries, and a few lesser-known beauties, like radicchio, New Zealand spinach, and sunchokes. While certain perennials, like asparagus, can survive for decades in some climates, not all will thrive equally well everywhere. I can't grow artichokes for more than one season in my harsh New England climate, for instance, while rhubarb is an excellent perennial choice for me. But if you live in Southern California—where artichokes grow year round—rhubarb grows as an annual.

What can be said about all of the following plants is that they're relatively hardy and marry well with regenerative goals. Although any plant can be grown using a soil-first approach, and be tastier and more resilient for it, perennials are a great choice because they require minimal to no soil disturbance. This makes it easier for carbon-capturing organic matter to build up over time. Perennials also allocate nutrients and energy differently than annuals and typically need less water, which is useful given how much dryer so many parts of the country are becoming. What I also love about perennials is how you always have a fresh harvest, even after a long winter. While I've lost plenty of corn to strong northeasterly storms, I've never gone a season without fresh strawberries.

The profiles that follow include suggestions and insights drawn from my personal experience growing these transformative crops. I've also tucked in a batch of favorite recipes. I'm excited for you to get out there and start gardening for the greater good. I hope it brings you the same joy I feel in growing my own delicious food.

# HERBS

# BASIL

**While primarily known as the main in-**
gredient in pesto, basil pairs equally well with
savory tomatoes and sweet strawberries and
can be enjoyed fresh, frozen, or dried. Basil is a
tender perennial, which means it can be grown outside
year round only in frost-free climates. It makes a good companion
plant for fruits and vegetables because the smell is strong enough to
repel bugs. Stick a sprig in a vase of water and it immediately fills a
room with that wonderful aroma.

**Varieties:** Sweet Basil is the most popular variety. Camphor Basil is
native to Asia, with sweet-scented white flowers. Thai Lemon Basil is
a mainstay of Laotian and Indonesian cuisine, where the zesty seeds,
stems, and leaves are all used. Hoary Basil, an African native, has a
strong taste and is often used as an herbal tea. Tulsi, or Holy Basil,
is originally from India and often prescribed in Ayurvedic medicine
to relieve stress. Lemon Basil, or Wild Basil, is a cross between Hoary
Basil and Sweet Basil.

**Companion plants:** Growing basil among your favorite garden crops
like tomatoes, peppers, lettuce, asparagus, beans, beets, cabbage, eggplant, and potatoes is thought to make them taste better. The complex
minty, anise, and ever so slightly spicy aroma repels pests like aphids,

beetles, mites, and tomato hornworms. Plant basil in pots around the edges of wherever you like to sit to help keep away the mosquitoes.

## Where it thrives

**Regional compatibility:** This herb loves the warmth of southern summers. It grows as a perennial in milder climates and as an annual in regions with harsh winters, like New England and the Midwest.

**Optimal sun and shade:** Give it at least six to eight hours of sunlight a day. If you have long summer days, providing a little afternoon shade can prevent the leaves from becoming scorched and bitter-tasting.

**Soil type:** Basil prefers soil that drains well and is moist, but never wet. But this is a forgiving herb that prospers in most soil conditions.

**Resilience:** Once established, basil is drought-tolerant and adapts well to heat. I plant it in pots so I can move it inside when the weather gets cold. If given enough light, basil continues to produce leaves all winter long.

## Planting

**Best time of year to plant:** Plant basil in the spring and early summer.

**From seeds:** Basil grows well from seed and quickly reaches a height of two or even three feet. Sow your seeds one-quarter inch deep in an indoor pot about six weeks before the last frost. If you have warm spring days but cold nights, let your basil sprouts sunbathe for a few hours outside before bringing them inside for the night. Your plants will be stronger for the experience outdoors. Once nighttime temperatures climb reliably above 50 degrees, it's time to transplant your seedlings outside. Space them about one foot apart. If you decide to plant seeds in the ground rather than in a pot, wait until the weather is warm and then sow them about three inches apart and a quarter-inch deep. Keep the soil moist and weed-free until the plants germinate. Don't worry about thinning until plants are about a foot tall. Then remove the weaker plants, leaving robust plants every one to two feet.

**From cuttings:** Taking a cutting from an established plant typically works well. Sometimes I pick up a fresh plant during the spring plant sale at my local farmers market. You can turn one plant into many by cutting off a four-inch, unflowered stem (mature plants usually have about three to four stems perfect for cutting). Trim the ends and place them in a glass of water, changing it every week to keep it fresh. Watch new roots sprout in about a week if it's warm enough. Plant cuttings outdoors once the roots are at least a half-inch long.

## Growing

This herb's flavor peaks in summer, just before the plant produces small flowers. You can extend peak flavor by pinching off the flowers, allowing the plant to focus on growing leaves. If I have more basil then I can eat, I leave a few plants to flower because bees love them. Another way to maintain flavor is by trimming any old and woody stems. Woody stems are easy to spot because they turn brown. Basil also produces lots of seeds that sprout on their own, freshening up the basil patch with new plants.

**Weeding:** The most important time to weed is *before* planting seeds. Once your basil is at least five inches tall, add mulch around the base to help keep the soil warm, moist, and weed-free.

**Watering:** Water when the soil is dry to the touch or leaves begin to droop. Basil likes its soil moist, and flavor quickly deteriorates once the plant gets thirsty.

**Fertilizing after planting:** There's no need to fertilize after planting. Soil that is too rich zaps the herb of its flavor and aroma.

## Challenges

Basil is a tender perennial, meaning it can't handle the cold. If the forecast shows a cold snap coming, cover your plants with light fabric, or a floating row cover, to insulate them. Since basil grows well in containers, you can also keep it in pots and move it inside on cold nights. If your winters are cold, you can make basil act like a hardy perennial by just letting the plants go to seed in the fall. The seeds will sprout the following spring without you having to do anything to protect them from the cold.

**Pests:** Aphids, slugs, and Japanese beetles pose the occasional threat, but pests are not a big issue. It's fairly easy to control pest populations with insecticidal soap or neem oil. Occasionally, flea beetles will torment my plants and can be hard to control with organic sprays. A floating row cover works well to keep the bugs off.

**Diseases:** Black spot and root rot are a concern in damp or humid locations. Keeping your soil loose and well-drained can help prevent these diseases. Basil is also plagued by basil downy mildew, which forms dark brown spots on leaves. There is no organic control for this. That said, this mildew usually hits late in summer, so it's possible to get a good crop before then. Just harvest the leaves and save the seeds, and all the disease will do is shorten the growing season.

## Harvest it

It's fine to harvest up to two-thirds of your basil plant at a time, or you can pick leaves and stems as needed. I tend to pinch off the first three leaves from the top, which have the most flavor. Regular clipping and harvesting help keep the plant healthy and robust. I sometimes pick a few leaves just so I can keep them in my pocket, rubbing them to release their fragrance whenever I need a boost.

**Store:** Basil is best used fresh, pretty much as soon as it's picked. In refrigerators, it goes brown. For short-term use, stick a stem of basil on your kitchen counter in a glass of room temperature water, with the leaves above the water line. Change the water every week until you've used up the basil. If it's around long enough to sprout new roots, pop it in a pot of soil and enjoy basil right from your kitchen counter.

**Preserve:** Freeze basil in ice cubes or dry it by hanging it in a warm, dark place.

# Basil Sunflower Seed Pesto

One of my favorite ways to use basil is in this bright, garlicky pesto. Nutritional yeast adds rich flavor and underscores the zing of this herb. Yields 2 cups.

## Ingredients:

2 cups fresh basil

½ cup fresh parsley (de-stemmed)

⅓ cup sunflower seeds, pine nuts, or walnuts

2 cloves garlic (or 1 tsp garlic powder)

½ cup olive oil

¼ cup + 2 T nutritional yeast

¼ tsp nutmeg

¼ tsp salt, more to taste

⅛ tsp black pepper

Squeeze of lemon

## Preparation:

1. In a food processor or high speed blender, pulse the basil, parsley, sunflower seeds, and garlic until finely minced.

2. With the food processor running, slowly trickle in the olive oil until the mixture resembles a nice paste. Scrape the sides of the bowl for an even blend.

3. Add the nutritional yeast, nutmeg, salt, pepper, and lemon. Adjust seasonings to taste.

4. Use immediately or keep in the fridge. Press plastic wrap on top of pesto while storing to preserve color and freshness. Pesto also freezes well for later use.

**Note:** You can keep the parsley stems to use in homemade stock.

# CHIVE

**Known for its piquant flavor and edible pur-**
ple blossoms, chive is often used in landscaping
to repel pests. Related to the onion, chives add
mild onion flavor to any dish and are popular in
dips, egg dishes, and sauces. This versatile herb is
as low maintenance as it is delicious.

**Varieties:** Common Chive (onion chive) has a mild onion taste and
brilliant round purple flowers. Garlic Chive, with its star-shaped
white flowers, brings a subtle kick of garlic. Giant Siberian Chive is
the largest chive. It has purple pom-pom flowers beloved by pollinators, and tastes like a blend of onion and garlic.

**Companion plants:** Chive plants have no enemies so spread them
around. You'll add beautiful color to your garden, plus chive repels
many common garden pests, including cabbage worms, aphids, carrot flies, and apple scab. This makes it a particularly good companion
for parsley, cabbage, tomatoes, carrots, apples, celery, and other crops
susceptible to these destructive pests.

# Where it thrives

**Regional compatibility:** Chive can live virtually anywhere in the United States but often withers in extremely cold winters before regrowing each spring. In moderate climates, the plant grows year round.

**Optimal sun and shade:** Chive prefers full sun but tolerates partial shade if you want to leave your sunny spots open for more demanding plants, like tomatoes and peppers.

**Soil type:** These herbs grow best in rich, moist soil. I plant them under my fruit trees because the soil is heavy with leaf duff and organic matter, plus the flowers attract pollinators so I get more fruit as a result.

**Resilience:** This is one of the first plants to sprout in early spring, but it also grows in hot, dry climates as long as you keep it watered.

# Planting

**Best time of year to plant:** Aim to plant chive in the spring.

**From seed:** Start chive indoors six to eight weeks before the last frost. Sow at least six seeds in each pot, one-quarter inch deep, and thin them to four sprouts. After the plants are at least three inches tall, transplant them into your garden two to eight inches apart.

The tiny, black, triangular seeds can also be directly planted in the garden, one to two seeds in every inch of soil. Wait until the threat of frost has passed and the soil has warmed up. Keep soil damp until the plants have taken root. Chive can be quickly overwhelmed by weeds so keep the area weed-free. Since sprouting chive is easily mistaken for grass, mark the area to avoid weeding it out of your patch.

**From cuttings:** If you don't want to fuss with tiny seeds, cut off the white end of the plant, the part that's usually tossed after the hollow green leaves are minced, and dunk it in a shallow glass of water. Keep it in the sun and change the water weekly. Before long you'll see roots sprouting and be able to plant it in your garden. As with every herb, you can also dig up a clump of chive, roots and all, and replant it in a new spot. I got mine from a neighbor who had excess clumps and was happy for me to have some.

## Growing

Chives have hollow shoots that grow to about a foot in height. Each year you'll see chive clumps grow larger and, in late spring, fill the garden with lavender blooms like pom-poms. Pollinators love to visit these flowers. Divide your mature plants every three to four years, preferably in late summer, to give them room to grow.

**Weeding:** Chive doesn't compete well for space and nutrients. So every spring, add two inches of mulch around your plants—but not on them—to help keep weeds in check.

**Watering:** Water your new plants frequently. Once the plants are established, you can back off a bit to about once a week. This should prevent the leaves from becoming bitter. Underwatering by just a bit can improve flavor.

**Fertilizing after planting:** Chive thrives in soil that is rich with organic matter, so once a year mix compost into the first three inches of the soil around your plants. Avoid adding nitrogen-heavy fertilizers. As with many other herbs, too much nitrogen can zap chive of its already mild flavor. In fact, if your soil is healthy, chive probably won't need additional fertilizer.

# Challenges

Newly planted chive needs to be kept weed-free. Other than that, it's really easy to grow and maintain.

**Pests:** Chive isn't vulnerable to many garden pests. Onion thrips can be a problem but are pretty easy to deal with. Since they like to feed in large groups, I just turn a garden hose on them to knock them off plants. For large infestations, consider using an organic insecticidal soap you can pick up from your local garden center or online. Most soaps are sold as a concentrate and need to be diluted with water. Make sure to read the instructions on the label for the best result. I mix mine in a 12-ounce spray bottle so it's easy to apply.

**Diseases:** Allium rust is a fungal disease that causes bright orange spots on plant foliage. The rust can be a problem in wet and humid climates. Your best defense is to water the soil around your plants, not the shoots themselves. Also, allow air to circulate around your plants by spacing them out.

# Harvest it

Wait to harvest chive until the plants are at least six inches tall. Clip the whole plant about an inch above the soil line, three or four times a year. For the best flavor, harvest chive before it flowers, typically in May and June. I like to use the mild-flavored blossoms to flavor summer salads and as a garnish if I'm trying to impress my dinner guests.

**Store:** For short-term storage, refrigerate chives in plastic bags or other containers. You can also stick chives, cut side down, in a shallow glass of water and leave them there for up to a week. I tend to forget about what's in my fridge, so this way I'm reminded to use the leaves before they wilt.

**Preserve:** The mild onion-like flavor of chives doesn't preserve all that well. I prefer to chop fresh chives and freeze them in ice cube trays with a little water. But you can hang bundles to dry in a dark, cool place, or use a food dehydrator. Spread out your herbs in a single layer so they dry at the same time, and if you're using an appliance set the temperature to no more than 120 degrees.

## Chive and Parsley Hummus

I love the deep green hue of this hummus. This recipe makes a batch big enough for a dinner party. Yields 5 cups.

### Ingredients:

2 cans or 30 ounces cooked chickpeas

½ cup tahini

2 cloves garlic, minced

1 tsp salt

1 tsp black pepper

1 cup olive oil

½ cup lemon juice

¾ cup chives, chopped

¼ cup parsley, chopped

### Preparation:

1.  In a food processor, blend chickpeas, tahini, garlic, salt, and pepper until it resembles a smooth but thick paste.

2.  With the processor on, pour in olive oil and lemon juice, and blend until fully incorporated.

3.  Add chives and parsley; blend.

4.  Adjust seasonings to taste, then serve.

# LAVENDER

**A favorite of hummingbirds and butterflies,** this fragrant member of the mint family is so robust it can grow almost anywhere. While its scent is alluring to humans, it's repellent to deer. Lavender is drought-resistant, making it an especially hardy option for beginning gardeners.

**Varieties:** English and Provence Lavender are sweet and often used in cooking. French Lavender is so strong smelling that it's typically used in potpourri.

**Companion plants:** Lavender pairs well with vegetables because it deters pests, including deer and slugs. I plant lavender alongside thyme because they have similar light, water, and soil requirements, making plant care a breeze. Also, when grown together, they're irresistible to pollinators.

## Where it thrives

**Regional compatibility:** Lavender is very hardy and weathers well. While it fares best in moderate climates with light rainfall, lavender can handle rainy, cold regions if planted in very well-drained soil. Most varieties do not do well in regions with long, hard freezes.

**Optimal sun and shade:** Full sunshine brings out this plant's purple blooms and fragrance. Lavender is especially happy when planted in warm, south-facing locations that are protected from the wind.

**Soil type:** This herb grows best in well-drained, sandy soil—nothing too damp or fertile. If you grow lavender outside in a pot, make sure to prop the pot a few inches off the ground so it can drain or the plant might not survive the winter, especially in colder regions.

**Resilience:** Native to the Middle East and the Mediterranean, lavender is often used in drought-tolerant landscaping. It also fares well in all but the most severe cold weather. If you're growing in damp, wet conditions, keep the soil well-drained so the plants stay healthy. I grow it in the cement breeze blocks that make up the retaining wall around my greenhouse. The soil is just five inches deep, and I water my lavender only a few times a month. I love how little care they require and how many pollinators they bring to my greenhouse.

## Planting

**Best time of year to plant:** Plant this easygoing herb from cuttings anytime from spring through fall. If you're growing from seed, start plants in early spring so they have a full growing season to become established.

**From seeds:** Gardeners typically start lavender indoors before the weather warms up because the seeds take so long to sprout. Sprinkle the tiny seeds in your pot, and gently press them into the soil. Seeds need light to sprout so be careful not to cover them completely. Move your seedlings outside after the danger of frost has passed. Planting seeds directly into the ground is not recommended because it takes so long for them to grow they can easily be smothered by weeds, or forgotten.

**From cuttings:** The easiest way to grow lavender is from cuttings. Place a two- to three-inch cutting in a pot with moist soil and put it in a sunny location. Once roots begin to form or the weather heats up, move your pot outside. When the cutting reaches 9 to 12 inches, transfer it into the ground. Store-bought plants can be planted outside anytime between spring and fall.

## Growing

Lavender can grow to be three feet tall and regular pruning keeps it productive and sweet smelling. To prune, cut about one-third off the height of the plant and remove any faded flowers. After its second or third year of growth, this herb starts to become woody and brown at the base. Be careful not to prune plants all the way down to the woody stems. They won't resprout from these branches and will slowly die.

**Weeding:** This is a robust herb and weeds shouldn't be a problem once the plants are established. Mulching will keep weeds to a minimum. Avoid using hardwood mulches because they hold too much water. Instead, use stone or shell mulches to increase drainage and prevent root disease.

**Watering:** Allow the plant to dry out between waterings. Lavender needs very little moisture to thrive—yet another reason to love this plant.

**Fertilizing after planting:** Skip the annual layer of compost. Lavender likes its soil barren. By not fertilizing the plants, you'll produce lavender with the best fragrance and taste.

# Challenges

Lavender is incredibly resilient and has no real growing challenges. It does attract bees, which is good for pollinating your entire garden but not so good if you have small children or a bee allergy.

**Pests:** Conveniently enough, this herb attracts both aphids and their predator, the flower fly. This means pests are not a real concern for lavender growers.

**Diseases:** Root rot, caused by overly damp roots and soil, can be a threat. You can avoid it by planting in well-drained soils and being careful not to overwater. My general rule of thumb for healthy lavender is to keep it high and dry.

# Harvest it

If you grow lavender from cuttings, you can harvest it in about three months. If you grow from seeds, you'll need to wait for up to six months. Harvest the beautiful purple flowers as needed. Your lavender bouquets will be at their most fragrant if you cut flowers on a warm, sunny day just before they open.

**Store:** Fresh-cut lavender can be placed in dry containers around your home as natural potpourri. Don't place in water or you'll end up with smelly, mushy stems.

**Preserve:** Lavender is best stored by drying, which takes about two weeks. To dry, hang bunches of cut flowers upside down. For the best aroma and color, keep the bunches out of direct sunlight.

# Lavender Lemonade

A touch of lavender elevates lemonade into something special. Enjoy it on its own or use as a base for cocktails. Yields 6 cups.

## Ingredients:

4 cups water

1 cup sugar

2 T fresh lavender leaves

2 cups lemon juice

## Preparation:

1. Combine 2 cups water with sugar and lavender leaves in a small saucepan and bring to a boil. Remove from heat and stir until the sugar dissolves. Cover and allow to sit for at least a half hour.

2. Strain the lavender out of the syrup.

3. In a pitcher, mix 1 cup syrup with lemon juice and 2 cups water. Add ice, and add more water or syrup if desired. Garnish with a sprig of lavender and lemon wedge.

# LEAF FENNEL

**Fennel can be finicky but its subtle licorice fla-**
vor makes up for the effort, plus it's beloved by pollinators.
Unlike bulb fennel, which is an annual, leaf fennel is a biennial, which means it throws off anise-flavored leaves, seeds,
and stalks for at least two seasons.

**Varieties**: There are two options when it comes to leaf fennel. You can
choose between bronze leaf or green leaf. I like to buy a seed packet of
each and mix them together.

**Companion plants**: Fennel is allelopathic, which means the herb may
prevent other plants from germinating. Allelopathic plants release
chemicals from their roots, leaves, or seeds. Fennel seeds are toxic to
most annuals. Beans, tomatoes, and eggplant are particularly sensitive, so keep them at a distance. On the upside, the aroma and flowers
are intoxicating to insects and will draw pollinators to your garden.
For best results, try planting fennel in an isolated corner where it can't
bother other plants.

## Where it thrives

**Regional compatibility:** Fennel grows as a biennial, so it lives for two seasons in climates where minimum temperatures stay above zero. In colder climates, it grows as an annual. In some parts of the country, like California, fennel is actually considered a noxious weed. To prevent it from spreading, snip off the lacey, umbrella-shaped flower heads before they produce their wind-borne seeds.

**Optimal sun and shade:** Fennel loves to soak up the sun's rays and prefers at least six hours a day of full sun.

**Soil type:** Fennel likes well-drained, moist, fertile soil.

**Resilience:** This herb does not adapt well to dramatic changes in temperature. It's quite sensitive to frost, withering away in extreme cold. In hot weather, fennel is susceptible to bolting, which is signaled by the appearance of masses of lace-like yellow flowers. Fennel is fairly drought-resistant, however, thanks to its long tap root that can access water deep in the soil.

## Planting

**Best time of year to plant:** Fennel can be planted right after the last frost or in late summer when the weather begins to cool.

**From seed:** Plant fennel inside four to six weeks before the last frost is expected. Put two seeds in every pot. Once your seedlings are two inches high, thin out the weaker-looking plants. After the last frost, move your seedlings into the garden. Be careful not to disturb the roots or your fennel may bolt.

One way to minimize disturbance of this sensitive herb is to sow seeds directly into the ground once the soil has warmed up. Push seeds into the soil one-half inch deep, aiming for 10 seeds a foot. That way, if some seeds don't make it, you'll still have a good harvest. Fennel can get crowded as it grows and spreads, so thin out entire plants as you harvest, leaving the remaining plants about four to six inches apart. If you don't use a lot of fennel in your cooking, you may be fine with just one plant.

**From cuttings:** If someone you know has a mature plant, ask for a root cutting. To get a cutting, push soil away from the base of the plant and look for a root spreading outward. Take a pair of sharp scissors and snip off a three-inch section of the root, preferably thicker than your thumb. Plant the root in a pot about five inches deep and water it regularly. In no time you'll see new shoots pushing through the soil. Wait until the new growth is five inches tall before transplanting it into your garden.

## Growing

Leaf fennel is grown for its feathery, anise-flavored leaves and seeds and does not produce bulbs. It grows quickly. Expect to harvest its leaves within two months. Mature fennel can grow three feet or taller, so it's best planted in the back of the garden where it won't shade other sun-loving plants. Unless fennel bolts from heat, seeds don't appear until the second year. I plant fennel as a border because its yellow flowers attract butterflies, lace bugs, and other pollinators. But keep a close eye on it: fennel is prolific and self-seeds if left unattended. Remove most of the flowers before they set seed or they'll spread like crazy.

**Weeding:** The feathery foliage is easily mistaken for weeds so make sure you know what you're pulling out of the ground. Mulch once your fennel is more than five inches tall to prevent weeds and conserve moisture.

**Watering:** Fennel prefers a moist environment, so water it consistently to get the best-tasting leaves. If the top inch of the soil is dry, give it water. If it's the seeds you're after, stop watering after it blooms because too much water prevents seeds from developing.

**Fertilizing after planting:** There's no need to add fertilizer during the first year because plants like to settle into place before being pushed to grow. The following spring, you might want to add a little all-purpose 10-10-10 fertilizer to give the airy foliage a boost for its second, and final, season. But even this won't be necessary unless you notice yellow leaves.

## Challenges

Fennel tolerates a limited temperature range, so if the weather gets too cold you may need to cover it. When temperatures are expected to drop below freezing overnight, I cover my plants with a floating row cover. The covering increases the ambient temperature around plants by a few degrees or more, depending on its thickness. In addition to preventing frost damage, it can keep pests off your plants.

**Pests:** Parsley caterpillar eats fennel, so gently pick off these visitors as you see them. This caterpillar turns into the beautiful black swallowtail butterfly, which pollinates plants. So rather than get rid of them, try to move them somewhere else, and don't worry if you can't rehome them all.

**Diseases:** Leaf blight, mildew, and root rot can be a problem for fennel living in waterlogged soil. Keep your soil well drained by adding organic matter before planting. Also, steer away foot traffic, which can compact it in humid and damp climates. Reduce the risk of mildew by giving fennel lots of space to increase air circulation around the plants.

# Harvest it

Leaf fennel is ready to harvest early in the season, about two months after planting and just before it flowers. The cut flowers look great in the kitchen and dry well. Clip sprigs or cut the whole stalk to add fennel to salads, coleslaw, or dressings. The whole plant—flowers, leaves, and seeds—is edible. When I have company over, I dress up dinner by adding a few leaves. What I most appreciate, though, are the crunchy, licorice-flavored seeds, so I always let a few stalks go to seed. Once the yellow flower turns brown, you can harvest seeds by clipping the dried flower and shaking it over a shallow box. To prevent fennel from self-sowing where it isn't wanted, I tie a bag over the drying flowers to catch seeds before they fall to the ground.

**Store:** You can store unwashed stalks in a cup of water on the kitchen counter for up to three days, or put them in the refrigerator wrapped in a damp paper towel for up to five days.

**Preserve:** Dry leaf fennel by hanging bunches upside down or place them on a screen so air can reach all sides. Check the leaves once a week until they're brittle and crumble easily. You can also dry the seeds. This takes about two weeks. Leaves and seeds can be stored in an airtight container in a cool dark place.

# Cabbage and Fennel Coleslaw

Coleslaw spiked with anise-flavored fennel is a playful way to update a classic. Tossed with a zingy mayonnaise-free dressing, the coleslaw is a refreshing side to a BBQ lunch. Serves 6 to 8.

## Ingredients:

½ head cabbage, sliced thin

2 cups shaved fennel stalk

1½ cups shredded carrot

¼ cup olive or vegetable oil

¼ cup white or apple cider vinegar

1 tsp Dijon mustard

3 T sugar

Salt and pepper to taste
(about ½ tsp each)

½ tsp celery seed

2 T poppy seeds

## Preparation:

1. Toss together cabbage, fennel, and carrots in a large bowl.

2. In a separate bowl, whisk together oil, vinegar, and mustard. Whisk in sugar, salt, pepper, celery seed, and poppy seeds.

3. Pour dressing into cabbage mixture and toss to combine.

# LEMON BALM

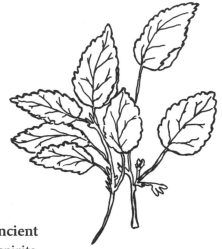

**Lemon balm has been used since ancient** times to calm the mind and lift the spirits. A member of the mint family, this herb has a citrusy aroma and grows fast. Also known as Melissa or sweet balm, lemon balm can be used to season dishes, flavor salads and tea, or freshen up a room in a vase of flowers. Another reason to love this perennial? It repels flies and mosquitoes.

**Varieties:** Lemon balm has been referred to by many names, including English Balm, Garden Balm, Balm Mint, and Melissa Sweet Balm. Citronella is a type of lemon balm bred to be high in citronella oil, which is used to repel mosquitoes.

**Companion plants:** This herb's strong aroma attracts bees and deters gnats and mosquitoes, so the plant pairs well with almost any fruit, vegetable, or herb. Tomatoes, melon, onions, cauliflower, broccoli, and cabbage are all good options.

# Where it thrives

**Regional compatibility:** This hardy plant can be grown almost anywhere in the United States, but winters where temperatures drop below 20 degrees can kill this plant. Luckily, lemon balm grows well in pots and can be moved inside before winter sets in.

**Optimal sun and shade:** Plant lemon balm in a spot that's mostly sunny but offers some shade during the day.

**Soil type:** This plant likes well-drained, sandy soil. Good drainage is the key to keeping lemon balm alive through cold winters.

**Resilience:** Lemon balm deals well with climate extremes and, while it prefers moist conditions, is resistant to drought. In very hot areas, plant lemon balm where it can get some shade each day so the leaves don't get scorched.

# Planting

**Best time of year to plant:** Plant lemon balm outside during the spring or summer.

**From seeds:** Sow seeds into small pots, or flats, six to eight weeks before the last frost. Since lemon balm seeds need light to germinate, don't bury them. Instead, just pat them into the soil. Keep the soil moist until they sprout. Once the sprouts have three leaves, transplant them into individual pots until it warms up outside. While planting seeds directly into the ground is not recommended, it can be done if you're careful to keep the area weed-free and moist. Plant seeds outdoors 18 to 20 inches apart.

**From cuttings:** Snip your cuttings from new growth or soft wood in late spring or early summer when the flexible stem is actively growing. Dip the end of the cutting in rooting hormone (while not necessary for lemon balm, this will speed up growth) and place in a pot of moist soil. Lemon balm roots very quickly so you'll be able to plant it in your garden by the end of the summer.

## Growing

When plants are one foot tall, they're ready to harvest. Since an entire lemon balm plant can regrow in about a month during warm weather, don't be afraid to cut back the plant when it gets bushy. To prevent too-rapid spread, cut off the flowers before they go to seed and weed out new plants each spring. Many gardeners like to grow lemon balm in pots as a way to contain it. In climates where lemon balm can survive the winter but temperatures drop below zero, put mulch around the plants in the fall to protect the roots from the cold.

**Weeding:** Weed until young plants are fully established.

**Watering:** Lemon balm becomes bitter when it doesn't get enough water, and it grows best in moist soil. This means consistent, down-to-the-roots watering. Even so, allow the soil to completely dry out between waterings.

**Fertilizing after planting:** Lemon balm grows quickly with or without composting. Since overfertilizing robs lemon balm of flavor, less is more for this plant.

# Challenges

You can keep on top of this fast-growing plant by continually harvesting and cutting it back. Another option is to contain it in pots so it doesn't spread where it's not wanted.

**Pests:** This herb has no noteworthy pest issues, but aphids and spider mites can become a problem when plants are underwatered. Treat the bugs with insecticidal soap, which you can buy from a garden supply store. Just follow the instructions on the label.

**Diseases:** Mint rust is a soil fungus that shows up in the form of small orange, yellow, or brown blisters on the underside of leaves. I deal with it by ripping out infected plants and replanting the healthy plants in a different place, where the soil is not infected.

Verticillium wilt is another soil-borne fungus that causes plants to wilt without warning. Infected leaves will curl, quickly turn yellow, and fall off. If you notice these symptoms in your lemon balm, remove the infected plants immediately and burn or dispose of them well away from your yard.

Yet another fungus to watch for is septoria leaf spot. You'll know you have it when circular spots with dark centers show up on older leaves. The best treatment is to remove all infected leaves. Avoid handling infected plants when they're wet so as not to spread the fungus to healthy plants.

# Harvest it

The plant tastes best during the summer right before it flowers. You'll know the plant is about to flower when the lower leaves begin to yellow. As with most herbs, the youngest leaves have the most flavor. Snip the leaves or harvest the entire plant, roots and all, and bring it inside. Keep it in a glass of water and the herb will stay fresh for more than a week.

**Store:** Lemon balm is best used fresh because it quickly turns brown, losing its flavor and aroma. To store, wrap lemon balm leaves in a moistened paper towel and place them in an unsealed plastic bag.

**Preserve:** Lemon balm can be dried in a dark, warm place but the dried herb won't have nearly the scent and flavor as fresh lemon balm.

## Lemon Balm and Ginger Cough Syrup

If you have a scratchy throat or a cough, this homemade remedy may be just what you need. Makes 1 cup that keeps for a week.

### Ingredients:

¾ cup water

2 T dried lemon balm

2 T fresh ginger, diced

2 T chopped mint leaves

2 T lemon juice

¼ cup honey

### Preparation:

1. In a small saucepan, bring ½ cup water, lemon balm, and ginger to a boil. Turn off heat and add mint leaves. Steep for 30 minutes, strain and set aside.

2. Add another ¼ cup water to the strained lemon balm water.

3. Stir in lemon juice and honey.

**Note:** Mixing when cool preserves the honey's healing properties.

# MINT

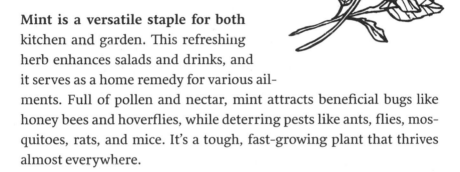

**Mint is a versatile staple for both** kitchen and garden. This refreshing herb enhances salads and drinks, and it serves as a home remedy for various ailments. Full of pollen and nectar, mint attracts beneficial bugs like honey bees and hoverflies, while deterring pests like ants, flies, mosquitoes, rats, and mice. It's a tough, fast-growing plant that thrives almost everywhere.

**Varieties:** Peppermint and Spearmint are the most common mint varieties, but there are others. Try the orange-scented Bergamot Mint or Apple Mint, Pineapple Mint or Chocolate Mint.

**Companion plants:** Plant mint near crops that could use protection against pests, like tomatoes, cabbage, kale, peas, and broccoli. But keep it separate from herbs so they don't pick up an unexpected minty flavor. I've learned it's better to save interesting flavor combinations for the kitchen!

# Where it thrives

**Regional compatibility:** Mint has few regional limitations but it grows best in areas that get plenty of rain. Still, this herb is plenty hardy and can thrive almost anywhere with the right support.

**Optimal sun and shade:** Mint likes full sun but also does well with some shade. Don't stress about the sunshine-to-shade ratio—mint is a fighter.

**Soil type:** This herb's native habitat is along banks of streams and rivers in moist, yet loose and well-drained soil.

**Resilience:** This perennial is fairly resistant to climate extremes and drought. It grows equally well in outdoor gardens and indoor pots.

# Planting

**Best time of year to plant:** Plant mint in warm spring soil for best results, but anytime before the first chill of fall is fine. In a colder climate, you can start plants inside and transplant outside when the weather is more forgiving.

**From seeds:** The mint family is large and cross-pollination hard to control, so your seeds may not produce the mint you were expecting. To prevent this from happening, buy mint seeds from companies that harvest from isolated plants. Sow seeds one-quarter inch deep, 8 to 10 weeks before the last frost. Seeds are slow to germinate, sometimes taking up to a month to sprout, and benefit from being grown in pots placed on a heat mat. Once seeds sprout, remove them from the heat mat and replant in larger pots until it's warm enough to move them outside, usually after a few weeks of sunny weather.

**From cuttings:** To start your own plants, you'll need one to two cuttings from a fellow gardener or a nursery. You won't need more than that because mint grows aggressively. This is why so many gardeners plant mint in buried pots. The sunken container keeps roots from spreading underground and popping up somewhere unexpected. If you grow mint outside of pots, space the plants 15 to 24 inches apart in moist soil.

## Growing

You'll have no problem growing this mighty herb, which makes it perfect for beginners. To keep the leaves clean and the soil moist, give it a light layer of mulch in the spring.

**Weeding:** Mint grows so fast weeds don't stand a chance.

**Watering:** Water every two to four days to keep it moist. Let the soil dry between waterings to prevent disease.

**Fertilizing after planting:** No additional fertilizer is needed.

## Challenges

Mint has a rapidly growing root system, which means you'll have to work to contain it. Otherwise the roots, also called runners, can quickly take over your garden. Control your mint by keeping it in pots or by frequent harvesting and pruning.

**Pests:** While mature mint is an exceptionally tough plant, young mint is vulnerable to snails, slugs, thrips, aphids, cutworms, and spider mites. Symptoms of spider mites include yellow or bronzed leaves and webbing that looks like a small spider web at the base of the leaf. You can get rid of mites by spraying plants with a strong jet of water.

Just make sure it's not so strong it'll hurt the plant. Cutworms are sneaky and will sever stems at the soil line, which means that by the time you notice the damage it's too late.

**Diseases:** Mint rust is a common problem. You can prevent this fungus from spreading by keeping plants thinned to promote good air circulation, and by removing dead stems as you see them.

## Harvest it

Mint can be harvested once the plant has reached three or four inches in height. Cut the leaves and stems with a sharp knife or scissors. If you want to harvest the entire plant, cut the stem about one inch from the soil. For the best tasting mint, pluck sprigs before the plant flowers. To extend the harvest, pinch off these flowers.

**Store:** Wrap mint leaves in a moistened paper towel and place them in an unsealed plastic bag. This will keep the herb fresh for a few days. You can also place cut sprigs in a cup of water out of direct sunlight.

**Preserve:** Mint can be frozen in ice cubes or dried.

## Fresh Mint Tea

Simple and calming, fresh mint tea is a lovely finish to a meal. For a deliciously sweet Moroccan-style tea, stir in sugar and serve hot. Or squeeze in a wedge of lemon for a refreshing pick-me-up. Serves 4.

### Ingredients:

4 cups water

1 cup fresh mint leaves

Optional: lemon, and/or honey

### Preparation:

1. Bring water to a boil in a tea kettle or saucepan. Turn off heat and add mint leaves.

2. Allow to steep for 3-5 minutes.

# OREGANO

**A staple in Mediterranean pantries, oregano** is flavorful fresh or dried and pairs especially well with tomato dishes. This aromatic plant grows easily without much water or tending. It's one of those herbs that makes gardening simple.

**Varieties:** Greek Oregano is the most commonly used variety in cooking, but Mediterranean Oregano is also popular and has a stronger, more peppery taste. Also delicious but not as hardy are Syrian, Turkestan, and Mexican Oregano.

**Companion plants:** Oregano attracts flower flies, which prey on aphids, so this herb is a good neighbor for any vulnerable plants, like tomatoes and fruiting shrubs. This herb's strong scent also deters cabbage moths from laying eggs on broccoli and cabbage.

## Where it thrives

**Regional compatibility:** Oregano can be grown as an annual anywhere in the United States. It's a perennial in places that rarely get colder than 10 degrees.

**Optimal sun and shade:** For best flavor, plant oregano where it will receive full sun.

**Soil type:** Oregano likes good drainage around its roots, so it prefers soil on the sandy side.

**Resilience:** This herb grows vigorously and requires little water, making it very drought-resistant and a good choice for first time gardeners. It tolerates cold pretty well, but if it also rains a lot, make sure the soil is mostly sand.

# Planting

**Best time of year to plant:** Plant oregano seeds indoors in spring before the last frost or outside after the danger of frost has passed.

**From seeds:** Sow seeds in flats 6 to 10 weeks before the last frost. The very tiny, almost dust-like seeds are easy to plant too deep. They need light to germinate so sprinkle them on top of the soil, then gently press them in. Once sprouts appear, thin the plants by moving them into larger pots.

**From cuttings:** Grab a cutting by snipping off a piece of an already mature plant. Make sure the piece is at least five inches long. Place cuttings into the soil 8 to 10 inches apart, cut side down, and water well. You can plant cuttings in a pot or pop them directly into the garden come spring. In a few weeks, roots should start growing and anchor the plants.

# Growing

Oregano grows two to three feet tall and has small pinkish and purple flowers. To keep it from getting too leggy, snip off the tips of the stems. This will encourage outward instead of upward growth. Remove any woody stems before winter, leaving behind the more flexible, light green shoots that taste better. Oregano can start losing its flavor after plants are more than four years old, so thin out the old plants that have mostly brown stems. Since it self-seeds prolifically, new plants will quickly make up for the loss. When my oregano plants get too large, I divide them in the fall and put some extras in indoor pots. Then I can enjoy the aroma all winter. In cooler climates, laying a bed of straw over the roots once the soil is frozen helps oregano survive the winter. Come spring, remove the straw to let the soil warm up more quickly.

**Weeding:** Tall weeds block the sun that oregano loves so much, so get rid of them.

**Watering:** Oregano is so low maintenance it doesn't need regular watering. Water it only when the soil is dry.

**Fertilizing after planting:** Aside from giving your plants a yearly layer of compost, don't fertilize oregano. Any added nutrients will only make it grow too fast and lose flavor.

## Challenges

Young oregano takes a while to get going. Trimming the plant shoots severely, down to two inches, several times during the first year will encourage more growth the next year.

**Pests:** The herb can attract aphids and spider mites, but it's so sturdy that in most cases you won't need to be concerned about pests.

**Diseases:** Oregano is not disease-prone, but keeping it well spaced will allow more air to circulate and help prevent mint rust.

# Harvest it

Harvest your oregano when stems are about eight inches tall. The more frequently you pick the leaves, the faster it will grow. Pruning also promotes healthy growth. You can cut an established plant until it's only two inches high at least six times in a single growing season. As with many herbs, flavor peaks just before the plant flowers, starting in late July.

**Store:** Keep fresh clippings in a cup of water on your kitchen counter for up to a week. Or refrigerate oregano in plastic bags, or in containers with a little bit of added water, for up to two weeks.

**Preserve:** Hang bundles of oregano in a dark, dry place. Dried oregano has wonderful flavor. Using a dehydrator is another good way to dry this herb.

# Tomato Sauce with Oregano

A helping of both dried and fresh oregano is part of what makes this sauce so delicious. Since good sauces are layered in flavor, be sure to season it at every step and use high quality ingredients. I favor fresh tomatoes but many cooks prefer canned because they have a lower water content. Serve with your favorite fresh pasta or layer into a lasagna dish. Yields 2 cups.

### Ingredients:

2 T olive oil

2 cloves garlic, minced

¾ cup chopped white onion (about ½ medium onion)

¼ cup red wine, optional

2 ½ T tomato paste

½ tsp dried basil

½ tsp dried oregano

Salt and pepper

15 ounces diced tomato

½ tsp red pepper flakes (optional)

1 cup vegetable broth

2 T butter

Fresh oregano, chopped

### Preparation:

1.  In a large skillet, heat olive oil over medium heat. Add garlic and cook for one minute, making sure not to brown. Add onion and cook for five to ten minutes, or until translucent.

2.  Add wine and reduce.

3.  Stir in tomato paste, dried basil, dried oregano, and a few dashes of salt and pepper.

4.  Add diced tomato and red pepper flakes.

5.  Slowly stir in vegetable broth. Reduce heat to a simmer and allow to cook for 15 to 20 minutes.

6.  Stir in butter or vegan butter, then add fresh oregano and season with more salt and pepper. Allow to simmer for a few minutes, then remove from heat.

# PARSLEY

**Parsley is more than a sprightly garnish. It's a** flavor-enhancer that happens to be high in vitamins A, C, and K, and it's also a good source of folate, and iron. I've gotten into the habit of sprinkling it onto soups and stews. It's a nice breath freshener, too. Parsley grows as an annual in cold weather and a biennial in milder climates. Its long taproot helps make this plant an especially resilient herb.

**Varieties:** Flat-leaf and Curly-leaf Parsley are the classic varieties. You might also consider Root Parsley, which looks like a white carrot.

**Companion plants:** Growing parsley next to tomatoes and asparagus is thought to improve plant vigor for both crops. It also helps roses by repelling rose beetles and makes flowers more fragrant.

## Where it thrives

**Regional compatibility:** Parsley grows best in mild, dry climates but can be grown nearly anywhere. If you keep it through the winter, it produces a crop in early spring. Add mulch to help it get through the winter if you live in a very cold region where temperatures drop below five degrees.

**Optimal sun and shade:** Parsley can thrive in partial or full sun.

**Soil type:** It prefers loamy, moist soil that's well drained.

**Resilience:** This herb does well in hot, dry weather and can handle most cold winter weather, too. It's moderately drought-resistant but will become bitter if underwatered.

# Planting

**Best time of year to plant:** If using seed, plant parsley indoors in the spring. Rooted cuttings can be planted once the weather warms up.

**From seeds:** For best results, plant parsley indoors about one-quarter inch deep three to four weeks before the last frost. Once they're about four inches tall, move your seedlings outside and plant them six to nine inches apart. Don't fret if your seeds take a long time to germinate. Parsley is slow to start, taking up to three weeks to sprout. Soaking parsley seeds overnight between layers of damp paper towels can help speed the process, as will setting pots or seed flats on a heat mat. Don't bother sowing seeds directly into the ground because it's nearly impossible to keep the soil moist and weed-free while waiting for them to germinate. Some thinning might be needed to prevent overcrowding as they grow.

**From cuttings:** Parsley can take root in water. Choose a four-inch long cutting with a good set of leaves and place it in a jar of water. Keep the water fresh by changing it every week or stems will turn slimy. Once the roots are a half-inch long, transfer the cutting into a pot or, if it's warm enough, directly into the garden.

# Growing

Parsley should be ready to harvest within three months or when it grows to be six inches tall. Remove flower stalks during the first year to keep leaf flavor strong and prevent the plant from going to seed too early. To help it survive very cold winters, add mulch in the fall.

**Weeding:** Get rid of any tall weeds around your parsley so it gets plenty of sun. Weeding the area underneath parsley will help ward off pests. Add a layer of mulch around your parsley every year in the spring to help prevent weeds from settling in.

**Watering:** Water regularly and evenly to maintain the soil's moistness, but there's no need to fuss too much. Parsley can manage dry soil for a spell.

**Fertilizing after planting:** Aside from an annual layer of compost, no additional fertilizers are needed during the growing season.

# Challenges

Once parsley is established, the plant is pretty foolproof. You'll love the bright green, feathery leaves.

**Pests:** Parsley caterpillars can nibble on plants before turning into beautiful black swallowtail butterflies. Gently pick off the bugs as soon as they start showing up, but don't worry if you don't get them all. The butterflies will pollinate the rest of your garden.

Carrot rust fly can chew on the roots of your plants but aren't a big concern because they leave the rest of the plant alone.

**Diseases:** Parsley that is crowded or planted in waterlogged soil can fall victim to stem rot and powdery mildew. Try not to overwater your parsley and keep plants thinned and well-spaced.

## Harvest it

Parsley is a biennial, so it goes to seed in its second year. When it sends up a flower stalk, it's time to yank the plant because the leaves have grown bitter. Before you pull it, let the seeds fall to the ground so that next spring new plants will sprout in the same spot.

Parsley is resilient and can be cut right down to the ground during its first season. The roots store enough energy over the winter that the plant can come back in the spring for round two. Parsley has a stronger taste during its second year. Once you take all the leaves you need, cut the plant at the base to make room for fresh seedlings to emerge the following spring.

**Store:** Store it in a perforated plastic bag in the refrigerator for up to seven days, or keep it in a cup of water on the kitchen counter out of direct sunlight.

**Preserve:** Hang parsley bunches upside down to dry. After three weeks, check to see if the leaves are brittle and easy to crumble. Store dried leaves in an airtight container.

# Couscous Salad with Parsley, Veggies, and Kalamata Olives

Inspired by traditional tabouli, this parsley-heavy couscous can be a stand-alone meal or a delicious side dish. I change out the veggies, depending on what's in my garden. Serves 4-6.

## Ingredients:

4 cups cooked Moroccan or Israeli couscous

1-2 small Persian cucumbers, chopped

½ cup roasted red bell pepper, chopped

⅓ - ½ cup chopped red onion

2-3 T Kalamata olives, chopped

½ - ¾ cup fresh parsley, chopped

1 – 2 T fresh mint, chopped

Salt and pepper to taste

2 ½ T olive oil

Juice of 1 lemon

## Preparation:

1. In a large bowl, toss together couscous, cucumber, bell pepper, onion, olives, parsley, mint, salt, and pepper.

2. Drizzle olive oil and lemon juice over mixture and toss.

3. Adjust salt and pepper to taste.

# ROSEMARY

**Rosemary adds a fragrant, pungent flavor to every-**thing from olive oil to vegetables and fruit. It does best in warmer climates and is drought-resistant. It also protects certain vegetables from pests put off by the plant's smell. Bees, on the other hand, love rosemary.

**Varieties**: Rosemary comes in many shapes and sizes, from seven-foot bushes to low-creeping ground covers. While all kinds of rosemary can be used in cooking, some varieties are more prized for their flavor. Popular culinary varieties, like Tuscan Blue, Blue Spires, and Spice Island, grow upright and have wide, needle-like leaves. If you live in a cool and damp climate, grow the Arp or Salem varieties because they tolerate soggy soil.

**Companion plants:** The strong smell of rosemary is fantastic at repelling pests like the cabbage moth, bean beetle, and carrot fly. I like to plant a hedge of rosemary as a border around my vegetable patch to keep these pests away.

## Where it thrives

**Regional compatibility:** Rosemary grows well in hot and dry climates. In northern regions where temperatures frequently drop below 20 degrees, rosemary will likely grow as an annual unless you bring it inside for the winter.

**Optimal sun and shade:** Six to eight hours of direct sunlight a day is what rosemary likes best.

**Soil type:** This herb thrives in sandy loam soil that drains well. Soil that is too rich or waterlogged stunts growth. If you don't have or don't want to cultivate sandy loam soil, water minimally.

**Resilience:** Rosemary is not a cold-hardy herb but it is very drought-resistant, particularly after it has been in the ground for one or two years and the roots have taken hold.

## Planting

**Best time of year to plant:** If you live in a warm, temperate climate you can plant rosemary anytime. If it gets very cold in the winter, start your plants indoors in the spring.

**From seeds:** Rosemary grows slowly in the first year, so starting from seed is only going to work if you're very, very patient.

**From cuttings:** I recommend beginning with three-inch cuttings. Plant them in pots indoors about six to eight weeks before the spring's last frost. After about eight weeks, your cuttings should have taken root and be ready for transplant. Transfer your plants outside when it warms up. You can also buy plants from a garden supply store and plant them directly in the ground.

# Growing

Rosemary grows slowly in the first year and then speeds up. If you have one of the large varieties, trim plants after they flower in the spring to the size you want. In the fall, you can take cuttings or divide the plants, repotting and bringing them indoors to enjoy throughout the winter. Add mulch in the fall to insulate the roots against the winter cold, and in the spring to help keep roots moist through the summer.

**Weeding:** Weeds can create problems, especially for new plants. Keep your rosemary weed-free to increase air flow and prevent fungal diseases.

**Watering:** Rosemary grows best in dry soil. In fact, once the plant is established, you'll need to water it only in times of drought, unless it's in a pot where it will dry out quickly. Whether your plants are in the ground or in pots, let the soil dry out between waterings because rosemary is prone to root rot.

**Fertilizing after planting:** Once established, rosemary won't need additional nutrients aside from the annual helping of compost.

# Challenges

A barrier to growing rosemary for the first time is its slow growth. Hang in there. Once it has taken root, this herb is pretty sturdy.

**Pests:** Mealybugs, spider mites, and whiteflies can plague rosemary plants, but the aromatic leaves do a good job keeping away most pests.

**Diseases:** Powdery mildew is rosemary's most likely assailant. In humid climates, root rot can also become a problem. Keep your rosemary pruned, well-spaced, and drained to prevent such issues. Most importantly, don't overwater.

# Harvest it

You can harvest up to two-thirds of rosemary at a time or just pick the leaves and stems as needed. Regular clipping and harvesting helps keep your plant healthy and robust.

**Store:** Clip off rosemary stems with sharp scissors. To avoid stressing the plant, harvest rosemary in the morning or evening when temperatures are cooler. Store stems on the kitchen counter in a cup of water out of direct sunlight.

**Preserve:** Rosemary's tiny leaves dry quickly and can be stored for use as a dry seasoning or rub.

## Baked Peaches and Rosemary

Baked peaches are delicious with ice cream or yogurt, especially when topped with a crunchy, nutty crumble and a dash of rosemary. Serves 8.

### Ingredients:

4 peaches, thickly sliced

2 T coconut oil

¼ cup brown sugar

¼ tsp salt

½ tsp vanilla

2 sprigs rosemary leaves, chopped fine

### Preparation:

1. Preheat oven to 400 degrees.

2. Grease an 8x8 glass pan. Place sliced peaches in the bottom of the pan, lying each one slightly on top of the next one.

3. Heat coconut oil, brown sugar, salt, and vanilla in a small saucepan until sugar is dissolved.

4. Pour the liquid over the peaches, then sprinkle with rosemary.

5. Bake for 20-25 minutes.

# SAGE

**While best known as a culinary herb, sage has** long been prized for its medicinal qualities, which explains why it's also called the savior herb. Its soft, resinous leaves have a strong aroma and their sweet, piney flavor enhances stuffings, stews, and soups. Tough enough to live through cold winters, sage can be grown just about anywhere.

**Varieties:** Culinary, or Common Sage, is best used for cooking because it's high in essential oils and flavor. Ornamental Sage is typically used to attract pollinators like butterflies and hummingbirds. This variety is also edible and the flowers make a nice tea or garnish. The taste of Tricolor Sage closely resembles that of Culinary Sage but the leaves have a splash of color. You can substitute Tricolor in recipes that call for sage.

**Companion plants:** When it flowers, sage attracts bees and other pollinators. So go ahead and pair it with beans, rosemary, strawberries, or tomatoes. Sage also protects cabbage and carrots from flying pests.

# Where it thrives

**Regional compatibility:** Sage grows best in dry climates but can be grown nearly anywhere. In very cold winter climates, add a layer of mulch after the first frost to help the plant survive the winter.

**Optimal sun and shade:** For the best flavor, sage needs full sunlight.

**Soil type:** It grows best in a sandy loam soil, but sage can handle almost any soil type as long as it has good drainage.

**Resilience:** This herb is extremely drought-resistant and does better in dry, hot climate extremes than in cold, wet weather. If you live in an especially cold and rainy region, your sage has to be planted in sandy soil that drains well. Adding pebbles as mulch is one way to keep the soil well-drained.

# Planting

**Best time of year to plant:** Plant sage seeds in the spring. If you use cuttings, move them outside once the danger of frost has passed.

**From seeds:** Sage can be hard to grow from seed, taking up to two years to reach maturity. If you do grow from seed, sprinkle three or four small seeds into a pot eight weeks before the last spring frost and gently pat them into the soil. Be patient because seeds can take up to three weeks to germinate. After they sprout, thin out all but one plant in each pot. If you want to speed things up, start your seeds on a heat mat set at 80 degrees.

**From cuttings:** Grab a few cuttings from another plant and pot them in soil. Roots will grow within six weeks. After root balls form, transfer the plants to your garden and plant them two to three feet apart.

# Growing

Sage grows in a round, bushy pattern. Promote fresh growth by pruning mature plants in early spring or after summer flowers bloom. After four or five years, sage starts to lose some of its aroma and flavor. You can improve the taste of older plants by cutting out the heavy, woody branches.

**Weeding:** Keep weeds to a minimum underneath the plant to prevent pests from taking shelter there.

**Watering:** Let the soil around your sage plants dry out between thorough waterings. If leaves look a little shrunken or wilted, don't fret. A little water will perk your plants right up.

**Fertilizing after planting:** Adding fertilizer can produce a plant with lots of leaves and little flavor. For best results, add a one-inch layer of compost each spring and avoid using fertilizers altogether.

# Challenges

Most experts recommend replacing sage plants every four or five years because they can become woody and stop branching. Woody plants do not produce the essential oils that give sage its wonderful flavor.

**Pests:** Aphids, slugs, and caterpillars can be a problem for sage but are easily treated with insecticidal soap or diatomaceous earth (DE).

**Diseases:** Sage is susceptible to mildew so avoid overwatering. Another tip: Water the soil rather than the plant. This reduces the chance moisture will collect on the leaves.

# Harvest it

When your plant is getting established the first year, pick just a few leaves. Either cut the stems or remove leaves individually. The new leaves at the top of the plant have the most flavor.

**Store:** Store in a container in the refrigerator for short-term use. You can also leave cuttings in water on the kitchen counter until they lose their freshness.

**Preserve:** Hang sage bunches upside down to dry them. After about three weeks, when they're fully dried, store the leaves in an airtight container.

# Butternut Squash and Sage Risotto

Sweet butternut squash pairs beautifully with earthy sage for this risotto, which I love to serve to friends in the fall. For an ultra-rich flavor, puree the onions before stirring them in. You can use farro instead of rice for a nutty, toasty spin. Serves 6-8.

## Ingredients:

1 medium butternut squash

3 ½ T olive oil

Salt and pepper

½ tsp cumin

2 small yellow onions or 1 large yellow onion

8 cups vegetable broth or stock

3-4 cloves garlic, minced

2 cups arborio rice or farro

½ cup white wine

2 T fresh sage, chopped

2 T butter or vegan butter (optional)

Cheese or vegan cheese

## Preparation:

1. Heat oven to 375 degrees. Chop butternut squash into 1-inch pieces. Coat with 1 T olive oil, 1 tsp salt, ¼ tsp black pepper, and ½ tsp cumin. Roast in oven for 40 minutes or until fork tender and slightly caramelized.

2. Thinly slice the onions. Heat 1 ½ T olive oil in a medium pan. Add onion slices, ½ tsp salt, and ½ tsp black pepper and cook over medium heat until caramelized, around 40 minutes. Stir frequently, and adjust seasonings to your liking. The final product should be the color of caramel.

3. In a medium-size saucepan, heat vegetable stock to a simmer.

4. Coat bottom of a large stockpot or Le Creusette with 1 T olive oil and set over medium heat. Add minced garlic and cook for one minute. Add farro and sautee for one minute. Add wine and cook for another couple minutes or until liquid is absorbed.

5. Slowly add warm vegetable broth 1 cup at a time, stirring constantly. You can turn off the heat at this point, as long as the risotto stays hot. Add salt and pepper to taste.

6. When the stock is absorbed and the rice or farro is al dente, stir in caramelized onions, sage, and salt and pepper to taste. Cook a few more minutes. Add butter or vegan butter if desired.

7. Toss in 4 cups of the butternut squash and serve hot. Save extra squash to use in salads, soups, or as a side for tomorrow's dinner.

# SORREL

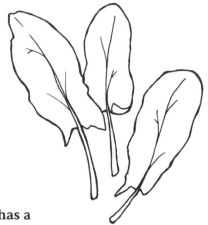

**A staple of French cooking, sorrel has a** tangy lemon flavor you wouldn't expect from a green leaf. This cold-hardy perennial is super tough and easy to grow in almost any garden space. It's known as an herb but is frequently used as a salad vegetable.

**Varieties:** Common Sorrel has green, arrow-shaped leaves with a sharp lemon bite to them. French Sorrel has smaller leaves and is milder. Red-veined Sorrel has bright green leaves with deep red veins.

**Companion plants:** Sorrel gets along well with just about everything. Plant it in the nooks and crannies of your garden where other plants might find it hard to take root. It's tough enough to grow almost anywhere.

## Where it thrives

**Regional compatibility:** Sorrel is highly adaptable and can be found growing along roads and in fields throughout most of the country.

**Optimal sun and shade:** This plant loves to grow in full sun during the cool spring weather, but it can get stressed as temperatures rise. In hot climates, the plant benefits from afternoon shade.

**Soil type:** Sorrel is not picky. It tolerates a huge range of soil conditions as long as it isn't sitting in waterlogged soils for too long. This opportunistic plant can grow in acidic soil with a pH as low as 3.5 and in alkaline soil with a pH as high as 8.5—a feat for any plant.

**Resilience:** This hardy perennial is relatively drought-tolerant but tends to get tough and bitter when stressed from heat. It can weather light frosts and cold nights, making it a nice addition to early and late season salads.

## Planting

**Best time of year to plant:** While sorrel can be planted all year, it's most tender and tasty when sown in early spring before the weather gets too hot.

**From seeds:** Start seeds indoors four weeks before the first frost. Sorrel has tiny seeds, so start them in two-inch pots using two to three seeds a pot. Once the plants sprout, thin out the weaker ones, leaving the strongest plant with room to grow. Once your plants have three leaves, transfer them to a larger pot while you wait for the soil to warm. You can also seed sorrel directly in the ground, planting the seeds one-quarter inch deep, once there is no longer a danger of frost. Keep the soil moist until the seeds sprout and be on the lookout for weeds.

**From cuttings:** Sorrel is best grown from seeds and not from cuttings.

# Growing

Sorrel spreads out like groundcover and is related to dock, a common weed, which means it can sometimes be a nuisance. At the end of the season, sorrel plants produce a long flower stalk with flat seeds that dance in the wind. Snip the flower heads before the seeds mature to prevent your sorrel from reseeding all over your garden. If you notice your plants becoming dense or bitter, dig up a few and plant them elsewhere. Or give them to a friend.

**Weeding:** Weed sorrel when it's young so it doesn't become outnumbered by fast-growing weeds.

**Watering:** Water deeply once a week while the plant is taking root. Sorrel needs less water as it matures.

**Fertilizing after planting:** Sorrel grows like a weed and needs no extra boosting.

# Challenges

Sorrel is one of the easiest greens to grow. The only problem with sorrel is that it can become hard to control. To prolong your harvest, keep it well watered.

**Pests:** Leaf miners are small white maggots that live between the two layers of a leaf's tissue. As the miners eat, they create winding tunnels, making intricate patterns in the leaves. Since they live in a hard-to-spot place, they can be hard to find and control. One option is to grow lamb's quarter as a host plant, then pick off the damaged leaves. This will cut down on your garden's overall population of these tiny flies.

**Diseases:** You shouldn't have any disease issues with these plants. In wet and humid climates, mildew can occasionally spread across the leaves. Keep plants well-spaced in humid climates to improve airflow.

## Harvest it

Sorrel is at its best in early spring and late fall. Harvest tender, young leaves for the sweetest flavor. Older leaves can get tough and bitter. Cut leaves from the base of plants with a sharp pair of scissors, and harvest only a third of a plant at a time. Allow the leaves to regrow before snipping some more.

**Store:** Sorrel can last in the fridge for up to a week. Store washed leaves in a bowl covered with a damp cloth. The moisture in the cloth will keep your greens crisp.

**Preserve:** Sorrel can be frozen for up to three months. Wash, chop, and seal it in a ziplock bag. I often stir the frozen greens into winter soups and risotto.

## Sorrel, Spinach, and Lentil Salad

In this simple salad, lemon-forward sorrel is chopped up with spinach and fresh dill, then tossed with hearty lentils and creamy avocado or goat cheese. Enjoy this tangy salad as a light lunch or dinner. Serves 4.

**Ingredients:**

1 ½ cup sorrel, thinly sliced

5 cups spinach, chopped

1 cup cooked black lentils

¼ cup fresh chopped dill

Lemon juice, olive oil

½ cup avocado or goat cheese

**Preparation:**

1. In a large salad bowl, mix sorrel, spinach, lentils, and dill.

2. Drizzle with lemon juice and olive oil. Add a few dashes of salt and pepper, and toss together.

3. Top with goat cheese or avocado.

# THYME

**Thyme is a fragrant evergreen herb that needs** very little water or attention. Dried or fresh, it adds a subtle finishing flavor to vegetables, soups, stews, and sauces. Another reason to love thyme? It will attract bees and other pollinators to your garden.

**Varieties:** Thyme comes in more than 200 varieties, not all of which are fragrant enough to use in cooking. Varieties that flavor food include French, Lemon, Carraway, Orange, German Winter, Summer, and English. Many varieties make a good groundcover.

**Companion plants:** Thyme is a natural companion to other herbs because most of them share the same minimal watering needs.

## Where it thrives

**Regional compatibility:** While thyme does best in dry conditions, you can grow this herb almost anywhere. Many varieties even do well in regions where temperatures plummet to below 10 degrees.

**Optimal sun and shade:** Thyme grows best in full sunlight. However, in hot regions it will only thrive with some shade.

**Soil type:** Thyme grows well in sandy loam soil. Soil that is too rich or waterlogged inhibits growth. If you don't have or don't want to cultivate sandy loam soil, use a light touch when watering.

**Resilience:** With so much variety, it's easy to end up with the wrong kind of thyme for your region. Here's where it pays to ask your local nursery for recommendations. Generally speaking, thyme adapts to extremely hot and dry weather, and it can grow well in wet and cold weather as long as the soil is well-drained and maintained. Because thyme grows best in dry soil, it is drought-resistant.

## Planting

**Best time of year to plant:** Plant thyme cuttings from mid-April to mid-May, depending on your region. If you grow thyme from seed, start indoors in the spring.

**From seeds:** The time to plant seeds is two to three weeks before the last frost. It's easy to plant the tiny seeds too deep, preventing sprouts from pushing through the soil, so add just a little soil once you've sprinkled your seeds in pots. Be patient. Thyme seeds take a long time to germinate.

**From cuttings:** Thyme is tough to grow from seed so it's best to start with cuttings or store-bought plants. Use cuttings from plants that have been grown in sand or dry soil and plant them in a pot. Once a root ball forms, move the thyme to your garden and space plants about a foot apart.

## Growing

Thyme spreads well, produces tiny flowers, and can grow to be about a foot tall. For the first year, prune lightly to help the plant get through the winter. After that, go ahead and prune as needed. You can prune by pinching off the tips of the stems. This promotes the growth of new branches. To help thyme get through the winter, apply one to two inches of mulch in the fall, after the soil has cooled but before the ground freezes. Many gardeners mulch thyme with a thin layer of limestone gravel to maximize drainage and suppress weeds. The lime also produces the more alkaline soil thyme prefers.

**Weeding:** Thyme doesn't handle competition well. Keep it well-weeded and protected so it can flourish on its own.

**Watering:** Water only occasionally, when the soil becomes dry.

**Fertilizing after planting:** Adding organic matter like compost or mulch in early spring can be helpful but it's not necessary.

# Challenges

In colder climates, hold off on pruning your thyme in late summer or fall. This only encourages growth that frost will quickly kill.

**Pests:** Spider mites can be a challenge in dry weather, dusty conditions, or windy areas with exposed soil. Spacing plants and pruning them regularly can help prevent a pest infiltration.

**Diseases:** Root rot and various fungi can develop in humid climates. Give each plant plenty of space and good drainage to help prevent these problems.

# Harvest it

You can harvest thyme whenever you want. As with mint, lemon balm, and many other herbs, you'll get the best flavor if you harvest in summer right before the plant flowers. Take as much as you want. Just about everything you harvest will grow back again.

**Store:** Refrigerate in a sealed plastic container or keep cut sprigs in a glass of water on the kitchen counter.

**Preserve:** Thyme has miniscule leaves that dry quickly. The dried herb can be stored to use as a dry seasoning or rub.

## Sautéed Mushrooms with Thyme

Thyme and a touch of white wine make mushrooms sing. You can stir these flavorful mushrooms into rice pilaf, omelettes, or pasta. Serves 4 as a side dish.

**Ingredients:**

1 T olive oil

1 clove garlic, minced

3 cups sliced brown mushrooms

¼ cup white wine

½ cup vegetable broth

2 T fresh thyme, chopped

½ tsp salt

¼ tsp pepper

**Preparation:**

1. Heat olive oil in a medium skillet, then add garlic and sauté for one minute.

2. Add mushrooms and wine. Reduce for a few minutes.

3. Add vegetable broth, then cover skillet and allow to cook until mushrooms are soft and the liquid has reduced somewhat.

4. Uncover, add thyme, salt, and pepper, and cook for two more minutes. Remove from heat. (There should still be some liquid remaining.)

# FRUITS

# BLACKBERRY

**Blackberry bushes can thrive in almost** any type of soil, making this fruit among the easiest to grow. These plants are so productive they yield fruit all summer long.

**Varieties:** Blackberries come in more than 300 varieties. Navajo and Arapahoe are popular varieties; both are thornless and grow tall, which makes picking the fruit easy. Cherokee is very sweet, but the fruit is harder to pick because the bushes are prickly. Blackberries also come in trailing varieties like the Olalli, which need to be tied to a trellis or stake to stand upright.

**Companion plants:** Blackberries tend to form dense thickets, making it hard to find a companion willing to endure the shade and thorns. Garlic and onions are good neighbors because their strong scents can deter pests from invading the bramble patch. Less companionable plants: tomatoes, eggplant, peppers, and potatoes. Blackberries are susceptible to disease and rot carried by these vegetables.

# Where it thrives

**Regional compatibility:** Blackberries are native to northern temperate regions across the globe. These berries grow so abundantly in the United States that some varieties are considered weeds in the Northwest, Northeast, and the Rockies.

**Optimal sun and shade:** Plant these bushes where they're most likely to get a lot of sun. They thrive on at least six hours of it a day.

**Soil type:** This fruit is not picky. While the berries prefer an acidic, well-drained, sandy soil, they'll grow almost anywhere.

**Resilience:** Blackberries can adapt well to both cold and warm climates, depending on the variety.

They have relatively shallow roots compared to other perennials, so they won't do well in long, dry summers. Watering is particularly important when they're fruiting.

# Planting

**Best time of year to plant:** Plant blackberries in late spring after the soil has warmed to 50 degrees. I recommend getting a soil thermometer.

**From seeds:** Blackberries are difficult to grow from seed, so the simplest thing to do is propagate from a few cut branches, or buy a plant.

**From cuttings:** To cut your own stems, or canes, snip up to eight inches of growth from a healthy plant. Do this during the fall when the plant begins to go dormant. New cuttings need at least three weeks in the refrigerator set to just above freezing. After giving them this cold treatment, put the canes in sandy soil and let them root, five feet apart, and keep the soil moist.

You can also snip off a piece of root from a mature bush. Take a two-inch section of the root and plant it in the spring wherever you want your bramble patch to grow. Monitor the root, looking for new shoots popping up from the soil. As with cuttings, plant roots five feet apart so the bushes have plenty of room to grow.

# Growing

The woods around my house are filled with brambles that feed a bustling bird population. I get rid of most of the new plants before they take over my fields, but save a few to replant along the fence line as a defense system against deer. Blackberries begin bearing fruit in their second year. After a cane fruits, it dies. That's one reason this shrub needs pruning at the end of the summer. Pruning is also the only way to manage the growth of this often unruly plant. Cut the fruit-bearing canes all the way down to the base, leaving four of the strongest and healthiest. This way, new growth will have enough space and sunlight to ripen the berries. If you want a natural-looking but less productive bramble, prune less often and allow it to mound up and spread out.

**Weeding:** It's hard to weed thorny blackberry patches once they get going, but it's also not a big deal because they grow like weeds and outcompete just about everything else. Mulching makes weed control much easier.

**Watering:** To produce a big harvest of high-quality fruit, blackberries require vigorous, consistent watering while they fruit. Once the plants bloom, give them at least a half-inch of water twice a week.

**Fertilizing after planting:** After the plants are established, they won't need supplemental nutrients. But if you notice your plants look lackluster or have yellowing leaves, apply a well-balanced fertilizer—a 10-10-10 mix should do the trick—or spread more compost around the base.

## Challenges

Certain varieties of blackberries are extremely invasive and should not be planted. The Evergreen and Himalayan varieties, for example, are ruthless and will suffocate the rest of a garden. These plants are nearly impossible to get rid of because they can regrow from the tiniest piece of root left in the ground. Ask your local nursery for advice on which varieties are most suitable for your garden. Another option is to plant blackberries in a pot buried underground.

**Pests:** Tiny beetles called borers can wilt the tips of blackberry canes. Prune back wilted tips to remove the beetle larvae and protect healthy canes from infestation.

An invasive fruit fly from Asia, the spotted wing Drosophilia, loves to lay eggs in soft berries. Within a day, little white worms emerge. These worms live in the fruit until the berry drops to the ground. Fear not this little worm. They're harmless and a source of protein if you eat them accidentally. Soaking picked berries in mild salt-water will make the worms float to the top of the bowl.

**Diseases:** Blackberries are susceptible to bacteria and fungal diseases. Cane galls are large growths or bumps that cause the cane to swell and split. Prune these galls and avoid planting cuttings from infected plants. Rust appears as yellow dots on the cones and leaves. It does not affect the fruit but can cause the leaves to dry out, so remove any canes infected by rust as well. Fruit rots are prevalent in mild, wet regions and can affect overripe fruit. Control this fungus by picking berries before they become overripe.

# Harvest it

Unripe berries have a dark red or purple hue and are so tart they make you pucker. Pick your berries when they are deep black. Harvest berries in long sleeves and pants to avoid getting scratched by these thorny plants. Bring a bucket or pail, and don't stack too many berries in one container or you'll end up squashing the ones on the bottom.

**Store:** Blackberries don't last long after they've been plucked from the vine, so try to eat them within three or four days. Store unwashed berries in the fridge to keep them fresh. Overripe berries are mushy, quick to mold, and will quickly spoil the whole batch, so toss the too-ripe berries in the compost.

**Preserve:** You can freeze berries arranged in a single layer on a baking sheet. Once they're frozen solid, store them in a plastic freezer bag. Frozen berries can be soggy once thawed, so use them for cooking or smoothies.

# Blackberry Gin Spritz

Blackberry syrup (or any fruit syrup) can be whipped together in a pinch and is a great way to use up ugly fruits. This thick blackberry syrup pairs well with floral-forward gin, but feel free to use it with just the seltzer, lemon juice, and mint for a refreshing afternoon mocktail. Makes about 1½ cups syrup.

## Ingredients:

*For the syrup:*

3 cups blackberries

¾ cup sugar

¾ cup water

3 T lemon juice

*For the cocktails (per glass):*

1 T chopped mint leaves

1 oz blackberry syrup

¾ oz lemon juice

2 oz gin

Plain seltzer

## Preparation:

*For the syrup:*

1.  Place berries, sugar, water, and lemon juice in a medium-size saucepan and bring to a simmer over medium heat.

2.  Gently prod the berries to break them down. Boil for 10 minutes.

3.  Strain through a mesh strainer to get rid of seeds.

*For the cocktails:*

1.  Place mint at the bottom of a highball glass and gently crush the leaves. Add ice.

2.  Pour in blackberry syrup, lemon juice, and gin.

3.  Top with seltzer to fill the glass. Stir and serve.

# BLUEBERRY

**Blueberries are packed with nutritious** antioxidants and vitamins. These plump purple berries are naturally sweet and juicy, making them easy to eat by the handful. They grow as a sprawling ground cover or an upright bush.

**Varieties:** Wild blueberries are impractical for most home gardeners. These low-growing bushes are a challenge to grow and a pain to harvest. I'm partial to them because they remind me of my childhood in Maine, but I generally recommend planting a taller, highbush variety, like Woodard Hombell. They're easier to reach and produce much larger berries. While most blueberry plants can self-pollinate, planting a few different varieties close together will give you a bigger harvest with better-tasting berries.

**Companion plants:** It's hard to find a good companion for blueberries because they prefer acidic soil. Consider planting your blueberries with other acid-loving plants, like hydrangeas and azaleas.

# Where it thrives

**Regional compatibility:** Blueberries are native to eastern states and can be found from northern Maine to the deep south. Wild type, or lowbush varieties, need cold winters to thrive, while highbush varieties are more versatile and easier to grow in both cold and mild climates.

**Optimal sun and shade:** Blueberries only need about four hours of sunlight a day to grow fruit, but the more sun they get, the more berries you'll harvest.

**Soil type:** Blueberries can tolerate a soil pH as low as 4.5. (Most soils are neutral with a pH of 6 to 7.) One of the biggest mistakes gardeners make (and I'm guilty, too) is planting bushes before acidifying the soil. Sphagnum peat and elemental sulfur are go-to materials for lowering soil pH, but they come with serious drawbacks. The mining of sphagnum peat and sulfur rock releases carbon emissions into the atmosphere and destroys natural habitats. Unfortunately, it's difficult to lower pH without these materials. Test your soil before adding peat or sulfur so you don't run the risk of using too much. In general, you'll need a two- to three-inch layer of peat or one to two pounds of sulfur for every 100 square feet to lower the pH by one number.

**Resilience:** Blueberries are not drought-resistant. They need a regular supply of water to produce a good crop. Wild blueberries are a great choice for cold climates with harsh, snowy winters but highbush varieties tend to do fine in most climates.

# Planting

**Best time of year to plant:** The best times to plant young bushes are in early spring, after the chance of frost has passed, or late summer in time to give the roots a chance to grow before the winter freeze.

**From seeds:** Plants established from seed take up to four years to produce fruit. If you don't have that kind of time, and I certainly don't, take cuttings or buy baby plants from a garden store.

**From cuttings:** In late summer, snip off the last six inches of a growing branch. Don't take branches that are actively flowering or fruiting; you want your cutting to have enough energy to develop roots. Place the twig two inches deep in a potting mix that is mostly sand. Keep the soil moist but never soggy and your cutting will take root by the following spring. You'll know it has dug in if you give the twig a gentle tug and it holds firm.

# Growing

Even if your blueberry plant is one of the self-pollinating varieties, some cross-pollinating plants yield bigger and juicier berries. So plant at least two different varieties close enough together that pollinators can carry pollen between them. You'll also want to pick off the blossoms during the first year of growth. Hard as it may be to remove pretty flowers, doing so helps the bushes focus on developing a healthy root system so they can produce juicier blueberries the following year.

Mulch annually with an acidic mulch like sawdust, pine needles, or pine bark. Highbush blueberries require different care than low bush varieties.

- **Highbush:** Since the biggest and juiciest berries grow on young branches of highbush varieties, you'll want to prune those bushes every few years. Get rid of branches that are dead, broken, diseased, or older than seven years.

- **Lowbush:** These also need to be pruned so they keep producing fruit. Every few years in the fall, or when you notice a sharp decline in berry production, mow down plants after they've lost their leaves. The shock of mowing jolts the plants into producing more berries. Without it plants slowly decline. Commercial lowbush growers typically burn their fields every three years to keep the bushes productive and the weeds to a minimum, but I wouldn't recommend starting a fire in your garden.

**Weeding:** Weeds aren't much of a problem for highbush varieties, but they are for lowbush varieties so keep them well-mulched.

**Watering:** Blueberries crave water, so give them about an inch a week. Once they flower, from mid-April to late May, give them up to four inches a week. This may seem excessive but sandy soil drains quickly and bushes need a lot of water to produce plump berries.

**Fertilizing after planting:** Fertilize blueberries in early spring before the new leaves grow. Use a nitrogen-rich organic fertilizer with a low pH, like cottonseed meal. Blueberries are prone to iron and magnesium deficiencies, so if you notice leaves turning a reddish yellow along the edge or if the leaves turn yellow but still have green veins, the plants need nutrients. You might want to mix a helping of Epsom salt into the first inch of soil; use one-quarter cup for every 25 square feet.

## Challenges

Keeping the soil acidic enough for blueberries can be a challenge. Depending on the quality of your native soil, it can take up to two years of treatment with sulfur to get the pH to the desired range of 5.0 to 5.2. To lower soil pH, I recommend choosing either sulfur or peat and simply following the instructions on the label.

If you'd rather not have to manage the soil pH each year, grow your berries in a container with one part peat moss, one part pine bark, and one part sand instead of soil. Another option is to buy an organic acidic potting soil mix. Keep in mind that bushes grown in containers need a lot more water and added nutrients than in-ground bushes.

**Pests:** Blueberries are prime snacking material for many animals and birds. Good fencing, netting, and a watchful eye should help limit the damage. The scale insect can also be a problem. Scale looks like raised bumps on new twigs and produces a sooty residue on leaves and stems. While scale won't kill your plants, it will weaken them, making them prone to other diseases. Control it by spraying a solution of neem oil or scrubbing them off with a toothbrush. If you have extremely infested branches, prune them. Spotted wing Drosophila is another worrisome pest for most fruit growers. One good way to control it is to clean up fallen fruit.

**Diseases:** In the fall, remove any fallen fruit to reduce the risk of fungal diseases. Ground fruits infected with mummy berry send out spores in the early spring that can blacken and kill new growth.

## Harvest it

Perfectly ripe blueberries are deep blue with a dusty coat. For lowbush varieties, use a harvesting rake to scoop berries from the foliage. Highbush varieties can be picked by hand. Try to keep picked berries out of the sun so they won't spoil as quickly.

**Store:** Blueberries are best eaten fresh or baked in desserts like scones or crisps. Or pancakes! To store blueberries, add a paper towel to the bottom of a bowl to absorb extra moisture so they won't get moldy as quickly. Keep them on the bottom shelf of the fridge to prevent cold damage.

**Preserve:** You can freeze blueberries for up to a year. Use your supply of frozen berries to perk up smoothies and baked goods.

# My Mom's Blueberry Cornmeal Pancakes

Cornmeal and fresh blueberries add texture to this breakfast treat. Serve with maple syrup or a blueberry compote. Makes about 10 pancakes.

## Ingredients:

1¼ cups flour

¾ cup cornmeal

2 T sugar

½ tsp salt

2 eggs

1 ¾ cups milk

2 T melted butter or vegetable oil

1 tsp vanilla

1 T maple syrup

2 cup blueberries

## Preparation:

1.  In a large bowl, whisk together flour, cornmeal, sugar, and salt.

2.  Whisk in eggs.

3.  Stir in milk, butter or oil, vanilla, and maple syrup.

4.  Lightly grease a cast iron skillet or frying pan and set on stove over medium heat. Pour ¼ cup of the batter in the hot skillet, then sprinkle on a handful of blueberries.

5.  Cook for 1 to 1½ minutes, then flip and cook the other side for another minute. Repeat to make the full batch.

# CURRANT

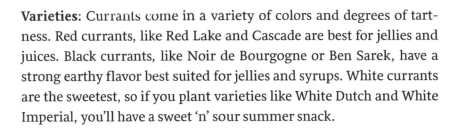

**This fast-growing shrub produces** many handfuls of sour berries in shades of deep purple, ruby-red, and golden white. Currants thrive for up to 15 years and are easy to grow. Enjoy these little gems fresh, or make them into a delicious jelly or chutney.

**Varieties**: Currants come in a variety of colors and degrees of tartness. Red currants, like Red Lake and Cascade are best for jellies and juices. Black currants, like Noir de Bourgogne or Ben Sarek, have a strong earthy flavor best suited for jellies and syrups. White currants are the sweetest, so if you plant varieties like White Dutch and White Imperial, you'll have a sweet 'n' sour summer snack.

**Companion plants:** Gooseberry bushes make nice companions because they share soil and water preferences. It's probably best not to plant currants, particularly black ones, near groves of white pine. This tree can carry white pine blister rust, a harmful fungus that will devastate your shrubs. Even worse, currants serve as an alternate host for the fungus. Some states have outlawed planting currants to keep pine forests safe from the spread of disease, so check to see whether they're allowed where you live.

# Where it thrives

**Regional compatibility:** Currants grow in cold midwestern and northern states as well as in areas with milder climates.

**Optimal sun and shade:** Currants aren't picky when it comes to sunlight. You can plant them in full sun or partial shade. In warm climates, currants benefit from dappled shade throughout the day, particularly in the afternoon.

**Soil type:** These berries grow best in a moist, rich, well-drained soil.

**Resilience:** Currants adapt well to the cold and can be successfully planted in states with winter temperatures as low as minus 40 degrees. The plants are less forgiving in extremely hot or dry conditions, and too much heat or direct sunlight can damage the berries. In hot climates, currants do better when planted so they get sunlight from the north and have shade to the south.

# Planting

**Best time of year to plant:** In the spring before the last frost of the season.

**From seeds:** It's very hard to get currant seeds to germinate, so they're rarely grown this way. I recommend buying a plant to get started.

**From cuttings:** If you have a friend or neighbor with an established plant, ask for a cutting. Cut sprigs in the early spring from branches at least a year old. Dip the cut end of each cutting into willow extract. While roots can grow on their own, it can take a long time. Willow extract speeds up the process so you'll be able to transplant your new shrubs into your fall garden. Place the cuttings in a pot cut side down and cover at least four inches of the stem with soil. When you move the shrubs into your garden, plant them at least five feet apart. The newly rooted twigs may look small, but in a few years you'll have large shrubs dripping with berries.

## Growing

As your currant plants grow, be sure to prune them. Cutting out broken and old branches that have stopped flowering minimizes the risk of disease and promotes new growth and healthy berries. Berries also have a harder time ripening in the shade of a dense canopy of unpruned bushes. Aim to have 6 to 12 healthy branches on every plant. Berries appear on second, third, and fourth year growth, so for the best results, try to preserve branches of different ages.

**Weeding:** Established shrubs aren't bothered by weeds because the dense foliage blocks the light they need to grow. But tall grasses growing around your plants increase the risk of pest invasion. Use clippers or a weed whacker a few times a year to cut back the grass. As always, mulching plants will help to control weeds and protect your soil.

**Watering:** Give your bushes about one to two inches of water a week. Thirsty plants are more likely to have sunburnt fruit that quickly spoils. But don't overdo it. Root rot can set in if the soil gets waterlogged.

**Fertilizing after planting:** Once a shrub is mature, it doesn't need supplemental nutrients to thrive unless the leaves begin to yellow. If you see this, add a nitrogen-rich fertilizer, like blood meal, to the base of your plants.

# Challenges

Currants require little effort to grow. The only real problem is that they're beloved by deer, mice, birds, and rabbits. I've even caught my farm dog, Nimbus, snacking on low-hanging berries. If your yard gets a lot of traffic from critters, you may want to put up some netting.

**Pests:** Currant leaves are the perfect hideout for aphids, which like to suck on the leaf sugars. Small populations won't harm plants, but large numbers may weaken them. If you notice leaves starting to curl, spray the tiny green bugs with an insecticidal soap.

The currant fruit fly is another troublesome pest. It lays eggs inside the fruit and when the larvae hatch they feed on the fruit, causing it to fall off the plant. Control fruit fly populations by removing fallen fruit from the ground before the first frost arrives.

**Diseases:** White pine blister rust is a common affliction, which is why gardeners in affected regions should select a disease-resistant variety of currants. Infected plants have yellowish-brown bumps that look like sprayed insulation foam. Fortunately, it's easy to prune infected stems. Powdery mildew is a risk as well, particularly if currants are overwatered. It produces a white, dust-like powder that coats and dries out leaves. For small outbreaks, remove infected areas. You can treat larger infected areas with neem oil.

# Harvest it

Currants taste best when allowed to fully ripen on the shrub. Look for colorful berries beginning in June and continuing into July. The tart berries grow in clusters like grapes, so just snip the main stem. Most varieties ripen gradually, with the top berries in the cluster ready earlier than the bottom ones. Keep picked berries out of the sun.

**Store:** Fresh, unwashed berries can keep in the fridge for up to four days. They last longer if you store them in shallow containers so none of the berries get squished or broken. I like the tart berries layered in a parfait mixed with sweeter fruits, like strawberries and blackberries.

**Preserve:** Currants can be a little too sour to eat fresh. They're probably best enjoyed as preserves. Freeze your berries until you're ready to use them. A dehydrator is an easy way to dry berries, and dried currants can be used in place of raisins. Currants also make an interesting substitute in recipes that call for dates.

## Currant Yogurt Parfait

I don't know about you, but breakfast is what gets me up in the morning. Parfaits are artful, nutritious, and sweet, and make a great start to the day. Serve in a glass dish so the layers are visible. Serves 2.

### Ingredients:

1 cup plain yogurt

Honey or jam for drizzling

12 T Goji Berry Granola (see Goji Berry)

1 cup currants, sliced blackberries, and sliced strawberries

### Preparation:

1.  In an 8-ounce glass jar, stemless wine glass, or glass cup, layer ¼ cup yogurt, a drizzle of honey or jam, 3 T granola, and ¼ cup berries.

2.  Repeat. Make the second parfait the same way and serve immediately.

# GOJI BERRY

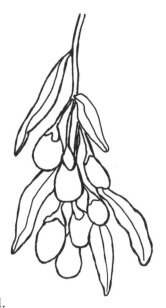

**Goji berries, also known as wolfberries, are** a member of the nightshade family. The goji plant is very low maintenance, so it's perfect for first-time gardeners who want to take a stab at growing fruit. These berries are packed with antioxidants and taste best when juiced or dried.

**Varieties:** More than 40 varieties of goji berries can be found in the wild. Most nurseries carry only one or two types so you may be limited by what's in stock.

**Companion plants:** Avoid planting these berries near nightshade crops, like tomatoes, peppers, and eggplant, because they're susceptible to the same diseases.

## Where it thrives

**Regional compatibility:** These are tough plants and can be grown nearly anywhere in the United States.

**Optimal sun and shade:** Goji berries thrive in full sun, preferring at least eight hours of exposure a day.

**Soil type:** They grow well in any soil except heavy clays that don't drain well.

**Resilience:** This plant is native to the Himalayas and adapts well to harsh conditions including drought, wind, and rain. In short, it's happy almost anywhere as long as the soil is well-drained and there's plenty of sun. Goji plants do not do well in waterlogged or salty soils.

# Planting

**Best time of year to plant:** Plant seeds and cuttings in the spring.

**From seeds:** Start seeds indoors six to eight weeks before the last spring frost. Sow them in pots first rather than directly into the garden where they can be quickly overrun by weeds. Place a few seeds in a pot with a mixture that is half potting soil and half sand. There's no need to bury the seeds. Just gently cover them with one-quarter inch of soil. Mist the seeds regularly to keep them moist but not wet. Once your sprout has three leaves, snip the main stem just above the top leaf. This encourages the plant to grow as a bush instead of a tree. Expect your shrubs to fruit in three or four years.

**From cuttings:** You'll enjoy goji berries sooner if you plant them from cuttings taken in late spring or early summer. Take the cuttings from the new growth because they'll root easier. Make sure cuttings are eight inches long with at least three sets of leaves. Dip the cut ends in rooting hormone before putting them in a pot filled with moist soil. Do not allow cuttings to dry out. If you can't plant them right away, keep them in a paper bag wrapped in a wet towel. Let your cuttings rest in their pot over winter before planting them in the ground. They can be planted outdoors as soon as the soil is warm enough to dig up.

# Growing

If not pruned regularly, goji plants will grow a thick mat of thorny branches that stretch in all directions. Plants can grow 12 feet tall and 6 feet wide if left on their own. Heavy pruning makes harvesting easier and encourages plants to produce more nutritious berries. So prune out dead, damaged, and diseased branches every spring. And during the growing season, prune back new shoots so the bushes grow out instead of up. Clip the top branches when they reach about four feet high. Don't worry about over-pruning—this shrub grows quickly.

Another option is to use goji bushes to help ward off pests. I leave my plants alone for the first few years so I can weave together the long branches to form a natural fence. While this means I may not get as many berries, the thorny barrier helps keep deer and rabbits out of the garden.

**Weeding:** Discourage weeds by adding a fresh layer of mulch under the plants each spring.

**Watering:** Goji berries prefer dry, well-drained soil. Young plants need regular watering to prevent the fragile developing roots from drying out. But once plants are established, there's no need to water unless there's a serious drought.

**Fertilizing:** These shrubs are used to harsh, barren environments so they won't need any extra help from fertilizers.

# Challenges

Not much can go wrong when growing goji berries. Fruits do occasionally suffer from blossom end rot, which is common in dry areas with fluctuating rainfall. If fruits appear mushy and brown at the bottom, they may have this rot. You can still eat the berries, but you'll want to cut off the rotten end first. Increasing soil calcium levels by adding gypsum can help prevent this problem.

Goji plants can be hard to get rid of once they have settled in. If you're not positive you want to keep them in the same location, plant them in a large pot sunk into the ground. All you have to do if you change your mind is dig up the pot.

**Pests:** Potato leafhoppers, Japanese beetles, thrips, and aphids can attack the leaves of goji berries, but these pests rarely pose a threat to fruit production. Birds can swoop in on your harvest, however, so you may want to net your shrubs after they flower. You might also try placing fake owls or other raptors around your garden. I've found that while birds are initially afraid of fake predators, they quickly get wise to them. So move the decoys around the garden to keep birds on the alert.

**Diseases:** Powdery mildew can coat the leaves of goji plants in the late fall. While this mildew may prove unavoidable in moist climates, proper spacing and watering can prevent it from spreading.

## Harvest it

Goji berries begin to ripen in midsummer. Bright red berries will dot the pale green foliage. Pick berries with care as bruised fruits quickly turn black and mushy.

**Store:** Fresh goji berries have a bitter, medicinal flavor some people love to hate. If you want to give fresh gojis a chance—they are highly nutritious after all—try them on cereal or in flavored yogurt, or mix them with something sweet to cut the bitterness. Fresh berries can be stored in the fridge for up to two weeks.

**Preserve:** If fresh berries taste too bitter, try them dried. Dried goji berries taste like cranberries or sour cherries and can last for a year if kept in a cool, dry place.

## Goji Berry Granola

Goji berries add a fruity punch to this granola, especially when paired with sour cherries and coconut. Feel free to mix in or substitute other ingredients, like hemp seeds, dark chocolate, or nuts. Makes 1 quart.

### Ingredients:

2 cups oats

¼ cup shredded coconut

2 T chia seeds

2 T coconut oil

2-3 T honey, maple syrup, or agave

3 T almond butter

½ tsp vanilla

½ tsp cinnamon

Pinch of salt

½ cup dried goji berries

¼ cup sour cherries

### Preparation:

1. Preheat oven to 350 degrees.

2. Place oats, coconut, and chia seeds in a medium bowl and mix to combine.

3. In a small saucepan, gently heat coconut oil, honey, almond butter, vanilla, cinnamon, and salt.

4. Pour liquid over oat mixture, making sure it's evenly coated.

5. Spread in a baking sheet and toast in oven for 10 minutes; then rotate pan to ensure even baking. Continue baking, checking every few minutes until the granola is slightly browned (it should smell toasted, not burnt).

6. Cool and toss in a bowl with goji berries and cherries.

# GRAPE

**The most prized grapes in the country** are found in California's wine country, but you can grow these vigorous vines in your own backyard, too. Eat them fresh off the vine, use them to create the best-ever grape juice, or try your hand at making wine.

**Varieties:** Grapes are typically either American or European. The American varieties are called slip-skin grapes because the skin easily peels away from the flesh. Concord and Catawba are among the favorites. European grapes have a very thin skin and small seeds, making them easier to enjoy as a snack. Popular varieties include Black Beauty and Ribier.

**Companion plants:** Planting hyssop among your grape vines will attract the bees needed to pollinate your fruit. If you're worried about pests, plant oregano and basil to deter insects. You can also plant a cover crop of legumes to increase the quality of your soil and produce bigger, sweeter fruit.

# Where it thrives

**Regional compatibility:** American grapes can tolerate cold temperatures, while European grapes prefer a hot, dry environment. Ask the experts at your local garden center which variety works best in your area.

**Optimal sun and shade:** Grapes crave the warmth and light of full sun. Fruit that ripens in the sun is the sweetest, so find a warm spot that gets plenty of light for your vines.

**Soil type:** Well-drained, sandy soil with a heap of compost worked into the ground will drain freely while holding onto moisture.

**Resilience:** Grapes tend to be drought-tolerant, but they're not invincible. Long dry seasons take a toll on the quality and quantity of fruit, and salty soil keeps fruit from fully ripening.

# Planting

**Best time of year to plant:** Plant cuttings in the spring after the last frost of the season and before mature grape plants start to grow leaves.

**From seeds:** Growing grapes from seeds is a long, rather complicated process. It can involve storing moist seeds in the refrigerator for about three months and tending to your seedlings in a greenhouse. (I've tried it.) So I recommend growing from cuttings or buying the plants.

**From cuttings:** Collect cuttings in the spring from plants at least one year old. Your cutting should be at least 16 inches long so it has enough leaf nodes to sprout new growth. Dip the cut end in a rooting hormone (I suggest using liquid or powdered willow extract) and place it in potting soil, covering at least four inches of the stem with soil. Anchor the potted cuttings firmly in the soil, pushing them in deeper if they appear top heavy. Not all the cuttings will root. Expect a success rate of roughly 70 percent. Once cuttings have rooted, move them into the garden and expect a fresh but very small harvest of grapes the following season. It can take three years before your vine starts to produce a noteworthy harvest.

## Growing

Grapes benefit from growing up a trellis, over an arbor, or on a fence. They need the support to keep from sprawling all over the ground where the fruit will be vulnerable to pests. It takes a while to grow grapes, which makes the first few years frustrating. Aggressive pruning, removing as much as 70 to 90 percent of new growth each winter, can help. Don't be timid or you'll have a plant that overwhelms a trellis or arbor and produces less and less fruit.

**Weeding:** Weeds aren't a problem for this climbing plant.

**Watering:** Water regularly during the heat of the summer and use mulch to retain moisture in the soil around the vines.

**Fertilizing after planting:** Grapes grow fairly rapidly in the spring. A high-nitrogen fertilizer will help them climb a trellis, but don't fertilize until a year after planting. Too much fertilizer can prevent grapes from producing the flowers that turn into delicious fruits.

## Challenges

Grapes have dense foliage, especially if not pruned back each year. It's not uncommon for leaves to shade out the fruits to the point where they can't ripen. If you notice your grapes are slow to ripen, pinch off the leaves that shade the clusters of fruit.

**Pests:** Grape phylloxera are tiny, aphid-like pests that can make leaves curl and bubble but don't harm the fruit. Japanese beetles are a whole other level of threat. These beetles have a brilliant metallic head with brown wings. They skeletonize leaves by eating the plant tissue between the veins. Large infestations can weaken grape vines, so treat your plants with a spray of eastern red cedar oil, which can be bought online.

If grapes start to shrivel just before ripening, examine them for signs of grape berry moth larvae. These pests leave webbing at the stem of the fruit and love to feed on sweet grape flesh. They can be hard to treat because they're protected from sprays once they enter the fruit to feast. The best defense is to watch for the brown-patterned moth flying around in late April to May, when it lays eggs on the leaves. Kill the eggs with an organic neem oil spray to head off the fruit-eating larvae.

**Diseases:** To avoid root rot and fungus growth, plant vines in a well-drained site. Certain molds and mildew can also attack your grapes, especially if you don't prune enough. Mold infections cause fruit to rot before ripening.

## Harvest it

Grapes start ripening in late summer or early fall, and tasting them is the easiest way to find out if they're ripe. If they're bitter or astringent, let them sit on the vine a little longer. Once picked, the fruit won't continue to ripen. So harvest the clusters when they're most colorful, plump, and crisp.

**Store:** Grapes can last up to three weeks in the fridge. Don't wash before storing. Washing grapes removes the protective coating, called bloom, that helps keep them fresh. Store the fruit in the back of the fridge where it tends to be cooler.

**Preserve:** Grapes freeze well. Toss a few frozen ones into sparkling water or cocktails and you get colorful ice cubes that won't dilute your drink. To dry them, use a dehydrator or put them on a parchment-lined baking sheet and bake at 225 degrees for about eight hours, or until soft and shriveled. Let cool, then refrigerate or store in a container for up to a week.

## Grape and Ginger Chutney

This thick and rustic grape chutney is full of texture and flavor. Fresh ginger and dried fennel give it a surprising zing. Use on toast, with cheese, or to mix up a PB&J sandwich. Makes 1 8-ounce jar.

### Ingredients:

4 cups black seedless grapes, sliced

½ cup sugar

1-2 T minced fresh ginger

1 T lemon juice

1 lemon, zested

Salt

½ tsp fennel seed

Fresh black pepper

### Preparation:

1. Place grapes, sugar, ginger, lemon juice, and zest in a medium pot. Add a pinch of salt. Toss to coat the grapes.

2. Cook over medium heat, stirring frequently to prevent scorching. Gently crush the grapes to help break them apart.

3. Continue cooking until the chutney starts to thicken, about 15 minutes.

4. Add fennel and a couple cranks of black pepper. Cook down for a few more minutes, then remove from heat. Spread on a baking pan to cool. Keep in fridge for one week.

# HUCKLEBERRY

**This hardy berry thrives in a wide range of** environments, from bogs to dry alpine meadows, and it can be planted right alongside your other favorite berries.

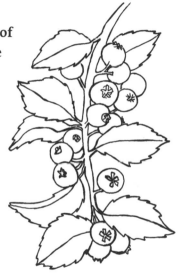

**Varieties:** The name *huckleberry* refers to a wide range of regional berries that stretch across the United States. In the east, Black Huckleberry or Box Huckleberry bushes can be found growing along blueberry plants, and the two are often confused. In the west, more than 26 mountain and coastal varieties span California, Oregon, Idaho, and Washington.

**Companion plants:** Grow huckleberries with other acid-loving plants, like blueberries. Planting them alongside a border of pungent garlic or chive can help keep deer from enjoying your berries before you get a chance to pick them.

# Where it thrives

**Regional compatibility:** With a little extra care, these berries can be grown just about anywhere in the United States, but head to your local nursery to find out which varieties thrive in your region. Whether you have wet, organic soil or dry, rocky dirt, there is a huckleberry that will work in your garden.

**Optimal sun and shade:** Huckleberries generally thrive in partial shade.

**Soil type:** Well-drained, sandy soil that is highly acidic works best. But you can grow huckleberries in almost any soil with the exception of soggy, heavy clay, as long as the pH is around 5.5.

**Resilience:** Huckleberries can survive drought, but moist soil produces the best-tasting berries. Depending on the variety, huckleberries are adaptable to both cold and warm climate extremes.

# Planting

**Best time of year to plant:** Early spring after the last frost.

**From seeds:** Huckleberry seeds can be started indoors in a pot, planted about one-quarter inch deep. Keep young plants in the pot for one to two years before moving it into your garden. And yes, this is a long time, so make sure the pot is big enough to allow for two years of growth. I recommend a one-gallon pot.

**From cuttings:** A quicker way to grow huckleberries is from root clippings. Gather four-inch root pieces in early spring and place them in shallow planting flats. Cover them with sand. Keep the sand moist and watch for shoots to appear. They'll grow pretty fast. Once you see signs of leaf growth, plant the shrubs in your garden about four feet apart.

# Growing

Huckleberries are slow growers, so you'll need to be patient. And unlike many other berry plants (we're looking at you, raspberries and blackberries), huckleberries should be pruned with caution and not until they're a few years old. Be sure to apply an acidic mulch like sawdust or pine needles each spring to help maintain the right soil pH. Shrub varieties have attractive foliage and make a superb hedge if you're looking for extra privacy.

**Weeding:** Weed before you plant and as needed during the growing season because these plants don't compete well with weeds.

**Watering:** The plant is drought-tolerant, but to produce a good harvest of high-quality fruit, huckleberries need consistent watering.

**Fertilizing after planting:** If huckleberries are well-watered, there's usually no need to fertilize. If you notice poor fruit production or yellowing leaves, you might want to apply more compost or a balanced 10-10-10 fertilizer.

# Challenges

Huckleberries have the same problems strawberries, raspberries, blueberries, and blackberries do. Animals and birds want some. Good fencing, netting, and the right organic pest repellent can help limit the damage.

**Pests:** As with most berries, aphids, thrips, and scabs pose a threat. So do rabbits, birds, squirrels, and other critters. In addition to covering your bushes with netting, you might try using Plantskydd®, which repels rabbits, squirrels, and deer by emitting an odor they associate with predators.

**Diseases:** To avoid root rot and fungus growth, choose a well-drained site for your huckleberry plant.

## Harvest it

The peak season for picking huckleberries is mid-August to mid-September. Ripe huckleberries are dark black or purple and dull. Pick them when they're slightly soft to the touch. You can enjoy them right off the bush.

**Store:** Huckleberries are not as sweet as blueberries, but they taste great fresh. You can store them for a week in a shallow container in the fridge. Do not wash before refrigerating or they'll decay more rapidly.

**Preserve:** Bake your berries right into a pie or freeze them to bake with later. Freeze by shaking them onto a cooking sheet and putting it in your freezer. Once they're frozen solid, transfer the berries to a sealed container. You can keep huckleberries frozen for up to a year.

# Huckleberry and Lime Jam

Lime and huckleberry are delicious together. You can double or halve, triple or quarter this recipe to suit your berry harvest. Makes 1 8-ounce jar. Store in the refrigerator for 1-2 weeks.

## Ingredients:

3 cups halved huckleberries

½ - ¾ cup sugar

½ tsp salt

Juice of 3 limes

Fresh cracked black pepper

## Preparation:

1. In a medium saucepan, cook huckleberries, sugar, salt, and lime juice over medium heat.

2. Gently crush the huckleberries to help them break down. Allow the mixture to simmer and thicken, about 20 minutes.

3. Before removing from heat, add a few cranks or pinches of black pepper.

4. Let cool before pouring into sterilized jam jars.

# RASPBERRY

**Anyone who has ever tasted a fresh-** picked raspberry can appreciate the joy of having a bush of ripe fruit within reach. Delicious in pies, preserves, and fruit salads, this nutrient-rich berry can be grown almost anywhere.

**Varieties:** There's a raspberry for every season. If you want your bushes to fruit early, try growing Prelude. Midseason varieties include the Black Bristol Raspberry and Encore. Fall-ripening fruits like Heritage can extend your picking season up until the first frost. Try planting a variety of plants so you can enjoy berries all season long. You don't have to stick to traditional red varieties either. These berries come in red, black, purple, yellow, and orange varieties, which all ripen at different times. I've grown a whole rainbow of raspberries just because I can.

**Companion plants:** Keep raspberries away from tomatoes, eggplant, peppers, and potatoes because they can make members of the nightshade family more susceptible to blight. Do plant them near chervil and tansy, which repel beetles that damage raspberry plants.

## Where it thrives

**Regional compatibility:** Raspberries are native to North America. With so many varieties to choose from, odds are you'll find a type that works for your climate. Since most prefer cool summers, raspberries are favorites in northern gardens.

**Optimal sun and shade:** Give the plants full sun for at least six hours a day. Raspberries grown in hot climates are happiest with some afternoon shade.

**Soil type:** Plant them in slightly acidic, sandy soil packed with organic matter.

**Resilience:** Raspberries adapt fairly well to both cold and warm climate extremes. They don't tolerate drought well because they need water to produce quality fruit. They also don't do well in soil that's wet or waterlogged. The key to growing resilient raspberries is well-drained soil in wet, rainy climates, and an annual dose of compost in hot, dry climates.

## Planting

**Best time of year to plant:** Plant nursery-grown bushes or rooted cuttings in the garden after the last spring frost.

**From seeds:** Raspberries are really hard to grow from seed. I recommend buying plants from your local nursery or digging up a few from a friend's garden.

**From cuttings:** Here again, it's better to just buy a new plant. Growing from cuttings takes a long time and the berry's roots are susceptible to disease. The reason I do it is because I get my cuttings from a family friend. His plants have been growing in my neighborhood for decades, so they're well adapted to the local growing conditions and need very little attention.

In late spring, I take eight-inch cuttings from mature bushes, soak them overnight, and dip them in willow extract rooting hormone before planting each one in a gallon-sized pot. The following spring, I plant the cuttings outside about three feet apart. You can also take root cuttings, ideally in late fall when plant growth has slowed. Dig out the base of the plant and look for roots as thick as a pen. Snip off a few and place each in a gallon pot, cut end up. If you're successful, new shoots will appear in a few months. Wait until your cutting has at least three leaves before planting it in the ground.

## Growing

Raspberries need lots of pruning to control growth and produce more berries. Every spring, cut out the dead or weak canes and leave 10 to 12 of the most robust. You'll also want to prune raspberries after harvesting them. Once you've gathered your berries, cut fruiting canes down to two inches from the ground. Tying your brambles to a stake will help keep fruit off the ground and make harvesting easier.

**Weeding:** Weed before you plant and as needed during the growing season. As with other shrubs, weeds aren't much of a problem.

**Watering:** Raspberries need vigorous, consistent watering to produce a good harvest of high-quality fruit. Mulch them each spring with straw, hay, or wood chips to keep the soil from drying out.

**Fertilizing after planting:** To jumpstart growth and promote plump berries, consider giving your raspberry bushes a balanced 10-10-10 fertilizer in the spring.

## Challenges

The biggest challenge with growing raspberries is that deer, squirrels, and birds all want the buffet you've so thoughtfully planted for them. Drape the plants in nets or use a safe repellent, like Plantskydd®.

**Pests:** Raspberry cane borers are tiny beetles that cause the tips of raspberry canes to wilt. To get rid of the beetle larvae, just cut off the wilted tips. Spotted wing Drosophila larvae can also colonize ripe berries. There's not much you can do to get rid of this pest, but removing overly ripe berries and clearing away dropped fruit can limit the spread.

**Diseases:** Powdery mildew can be a problem, so choose a site with well-drained, sandy soil and water only when the soil is dry.

## Harvest it

Look for deep red berries from June to September. Different varieties ripen at different times. Try to pick ripe berries during the cooler hours of the morning when they're firmer so they're less likely to squish in your fingers.

**Store:** Put berries in a shallow container lined with paper towels to absorb moisture, and store it in the fridge. If you plan to keep the berries for more than three days, mix a half cup of vinegar with four cups of water and gently wash away the mold or dirt that can make them go bad. Pat dry with paper towels before refrigerating them.

**Preserve:** You can freeze raspberries for up to a year. I freeze them in a single layer on a baking sheet and store them in airtight containers. Shake out as many of the frozen berries as you want for pies, jams, and smoothies.

# Raspberry Crisp

A fresh fruit crisp may be my favorite way to finish off an outdoor summer meal. In this recipe, juicy raspberries are topped with a toasty, nutty crumble. Serve warm with ice cream, or as a midday snack with coffee or tea. Serves 8.

## Ingredients:

6 cups raspberries

2 T flour

¼ cup sugar (white or brown)

½ teaspoon cinnamon

Salt

2 T lemon juice

Crumble Topping:

1 cup flour or almond flour

1 cup oats

½ cup brown sugar

½ tsp salt

¾ cup chopped almonds

¾ cup cold butter, cubed

## Preparation:

1. Preheat oven to 375 degrees and grease a 9x13 baking dish.

2. Toss raspberries with the flour, sugar, cinnamon, a pinch of salt, and lemon juice. Spread in a baking dish.

3. In a separate bowl, whisk together 1 cup flour, oats, brown sugar, salt, and almonds. Work in butter.

4. Sprinkle crumble over raspberry mixture.

5. Bake until raspberries are bubbling and topping is a golden brown, about 30 minutes.

# STRAWBERRY

**Strawberries may seem like annuals** when they wither in the winter. But in most regions they're grown as perennials and send out vigorous green shoots every spring. These bright red berries are delicious fresh, baked, or preserved in jams.

**Varieties:** June Bearing Strawberries produce one large crop in the spring. Day Neutral Strawberries produce smaller quantities of fruit throughout the spring and summer, no matter how much daylight they get. Everbearing Strawberries yield two or three crops of berries during the growing season.

**Companion plants:** Strawberry plants get along with just about every other plant in the garden, so take advantage of it. Plant strawberries near garlic and chive to deter pests put off by their odor. Plant near thyme to ward off worms, and near spinach to enhance productivity. Here's another tip: Plant your berries among leafy plants, like lettuce, and hide the ripening fruit from hungry birds.

# Where it thrives

**Regional compatibility:** Strawberries thrive in almost every climate, although where temperatures drop below 20 degrees it can be hard to grow them as perennials.

**Optimal sun and shade:** Strawberries love the sun, so give them sun.

**Soil type:** Well-drained, sandy soil is best.

**Resilience:** Strawberries need rain or regular watering. Optimal fruit-ripening temperature is somewhere between 60 and 80 degrees.

# Planting

**Best time of year to plant:** Plant in the spring if you have harsh winters. If you have mild, frost-free winters, plant in the late fall.

**From seeds:** Strawberries are hard to grow from seed. I recommend starting with plants or cuttings.

**From cuttings:** Strawberry plants are easy to grow from runners, the baby plants that spiral out from the main plant. If you have a friend with a strawberry patch, ask for some runners, which usually appear in the fall. Snip off these small plants and place them leaf side up on the soil, 20 inches apart. Press them firmly into the soil so they won't blow away, and they'll root on their own. If you live in a northern climate, keep them inside in pots for the winter. Come spring, they'll be ready to set outside. In warm southern climates, all runners will need to survive the winter is a layer of mulch. They'll grow into adult plants the following spring.

# Growing

Strawberries burst out of the ground in the spring and bear fruit one or two months after flowering. To grow strawberries as perennials, cover them with mulch in the fall to insulate them from the cold. If all goes well, your plants will send out fresh runners the following spring. Mother plants stop bearing fruit after four growing seasons so I always clip a few runners to replant each year.

**Weeding:** Clear your patch each spring to keep it from getting overgrown. I use straw mulch to curb the weeds and cool the soil. Straw also prevents the berries from touching the ground and becoming snacks for bugs.

**Watering:** Give your berries one or two inches of water a week, especially during the growing and harvest seasons.

**Fertilizing after planting:** These plants need nitrogen and phosphorus to produce prolific leaves and fruits. Help your plants thrive by adding a nitrogen-rich fertilizer like blood meal or a phosphorus-rich fertilizer like bone meal in the spring.

# Challenges

Their bright colors and soft flesh make strawberries an easy target for all kinds of critters. This may sound nuts, but I use berry decoys to distract birds: I paint rocks to look like strawberries and set them out. Curious birds will learn your fake berries are hard and unpalatable, and may leave your fruit alone—or that's the idea anyway!

**Pests:** This low-lying perennial is susceptible to slugs. Deter these slimy intruders by scattering broken eggshells around your plant or making a ringed barrier of diatomaceous earth (DE). The tarnished plant bug, a small flat insect with wings, can also be a problem. Pick off any you see or spray them with an insecticidal soap. The most formidable enemy for strawberry plants is the bud weevil. This insect has a long snout it uses to pierce new buds, preventing fruit from forming. Get rid of them by cutting off any infected buds you see.

**Diseases:** Root rots are common afflictions for strawberry plants. Minimize the risk of rot by picking a well-drained site, and don't overwater. Fruit rot, which appears as a gray fluffy mold, can affect fruits that touch dead leaves or the ground. Keep berries off the ground with mulch and make sure they stay clear of dead leaves.

## Harvest it

Harvest strawberries when they're bright red by snapping or cutting the stems. If you notice white areas around the berry, rotate the fruit on the stem so the pale side faces the sun and fully ripens. I check my patch daily once the berries start to redden so I can snatch up the ripe ones before the birds and bugs get them.

**Store:** Eating a sun-warmed strawberry fresh from the garden never gets old. And that really is the best way to enjoy them because they lose flavor rapidly. If you do have to store them, place unwashed berries in a shallow, breathable container lined with paper towels. Refrigerated berries should last a couple of days. Don't stack many berries on top of each other or you'll end up with a mushy mess.

**Preserve:** To lock in flavor, bag your berries after you've washed, dried, and removed their stems, and store them in your freezer.

# Strawberry Basil Jam

Strawberries and basil make one of summer's finest pairings. Stir this jam into yogurt or oatmeal, use on toast, or eat with your favorite pastry. Makes 1 16-ounce jar or 2 8-ounce jars. Keeps in fridge for 1-2 weeks.

## Ingredients:

4 cups strawberries

1 ¼ cup sugar

½ tsp salt

1 lemon, juiced and zested

1 orange, zested

2-3 T chopped basil

## Preparation:

1. Place strawberries, sugar, salt, lemon juice, and zests in a medium-size pot. Toss to coat strawberries, then cook over medium heat.

2. Stir frequently to prevent scorching while strawberries cook down and thicken, about 15–20 minutes.

3. As the jam reaches desired thickness, add chopped basil. Cook for a few more minutes, then remove from heat.

4. Let cool before pouring into sterilized jam jars.

# VEGETABLES

# ARTICHOKE

**Artichokes are grown for their edible immature flower buds. If** you leave a few to bloom, the bright purple, thistle-like flowers will attract hummingbirds. While not terribly adaptable, artichokes are salt-tolerant, which makes them a favorite of coastal gardeners in mild climates.

**Varieties:** Globe artichokes come in different shapes and sizes. Common round varieties include Green Globe and Imperial Star. Less spherical, elongated artichoke varieties include the popular Violetto. Purple varieties like Fiesole can add a splash of color to your plate and garden.

**Companion plants:** Traditional companion planting isn't always desirable for artichokes because they're quite large and cast a lot of shade. I've had success pairing them with peas because they share the same soil preference. Peas also produce nitrogen, which benefits the artichokes. Sunflowers can be good neighbors, too, because they're part of the same family, though they compete for sunlight.

# Where it thrives

**Regional compatibility:** Artichokes grow well in most parts of the country but do best in western coastal regions, like the central coast of California. Gardeners who live in areas where temperatures drop below zero will want to grow annuals, like Imperial Star or Colorado Star, which can be harvested in 90 days. Perennial artichokes need a full growing season before they'll bud.

**Optimal sun and shade:** Artichokes grow best in full sun.

**Soil type:** Artichokes need sandy loam packed with nutrients. They won't do well in soil that gets waterlogged, so if you have clay soil, work in some sand and organic matter to improve drainage. You can also plant them on a raised mound.

**Resilience:** These vegetables prefer moderate temperatures and don't do as well in climate extremes. Intense cold snaps can damage their roots and very hot summers sap them of energy. Artichokes tolerate water stress, but at the expense of tenderness because thirsty plants bud prematurely. The only artichokes that can be grown using very little water are ornamental, not food crops.

# Planting

**Best time of year to plant:** If you live in an area with a cold winter, spring is the best option. Otherwise, fall is a fine time to plant, too.

**From seeds:** Starting seeds indoors, preferably 8 to 12 weeks before the beginning of summer, is recommended for a quicker harvest. Push two to three seeds one-quarter inch deep in a pot of soil. Using more than one seed will improve the odds you'll get at least one artichoke in every pot. Place your pots or flats on a heat mat because artichoke seeds like soil temperatures between 70 and 80 degrees. As soon as your seedlings have three leaves, thin out all but the biggest ones by snipping them off at the base with scissors. Transplant seedlings outdoors once nighttime temperatures hit the 50s. Since they can grow to be very large, set seedlings at least three feet apart. If you plant seeds directly in your garden, wait until the soil has warmed to at least 60 degrees. I use a soil thermometer to gauge heat. Perennial artichokes seeded directly outdoors may not produce buds during the first growing season. A simpler way to start this vegetable is to dig up a few from a friend's garden and replant them in yours.

**From cuttings:** Artichokes often produce side shoots that grow alongside the central stalk. If you take great care not to damage the central stem, you can cut away the side shoots, dig them up, and plant them. To get your cuttings, place a serrated knife between the central stalk and the side shoot at soil level. Cut close to the side shoot, sawing back and forth to separate the side shoot roots from those of the central stem. Then insert a trowel six to eight inches deep in the soil around the side shoot. Pull up the side shoot while lifting the trowel. This should free it with minimum damage to the central stalk. If the side shoot doesn't come up in one go, sink the trowel into a different spot and try again.

Once you've freed the shoot, dig a hole twice as big as the root mass and replant, taking care to mix in compost before you do. Spread out the roots before covering them back up with soil.

## Growing

Artichokes have beautiful silver foliage and can grow as big as four feet tall and five feet wide. They are at their peak in early summer and produce a second harvest of side shoot buds in midsummer. Artichokes may need to be staked once a bud forms because they can become top heavy. To secure an artichoke, push a bamboo stake into the ground at the base of the plant. Use landscaping yarn or old strips of T-shirts to tie the plant to the pole. Be careful not to tie it too tight or it will girdle or choke itself. Water and nutrients won't be able flow from the roots to the leaves.

Pruning is unnecessary for healthy plants, but do remove the bottom leaves if they begin to wilt to prevent mildew outbreaks. Spreading a thick mat of straw over your artichoke crowns can help insulate them in the winter.

**Weeding:** Keep artichoke beds weed-free from the start.

**Watering:** Water every two days in the important early stages when flowers are budding. Mature artichokes need one or two inches of water a week. Let the soil dry out between waterings so it doesn't get soggy.

**Fertilizing after planting:** Artichokes are heavy feeders so mix in at least two inches of compost when planting. If your soil requires additional nutrients, use a nitrogen-heavy fertilizer, like blood meal or composted manure.

## Challenges

Artichokes do not like extreme cold. If you live where winters can get harsh, mulch your plants in the fall during the first year or two when they're most susceptible to frost.

**Pests:** The artichoke's robust foliage can hide irksome pests like aphids and spittlebug larvae that feed on the supple buds and leaves. Pick or hose off these bugs. They'll affect the quality of the artichokes but only if there are lots of them.

Slugs and snails often feed on artichokes but won't cause much damage. Spread some crushed eggshells or diatomaceous earth (DE) in a circle around the base of the plant to prevent these slimy invaders from climbing up the stems and into the leaves.

**Diseases:** Curly dwarf virus, which is spread by aphids, can stunt growth or produce misshapen artichokes. To prevent the spread of this virus, get rid of any milk thistle that might be growing nearby and try to control aphids as soon as you see them. You can recognize aphids by their pear-shaped body and lice-like appearance. There is no cure for the virus they cause, so you'll have to toss infected artichokes in the garbage rather than compost them.

Powdery mildew, verticillium wilt, and botrytis rot are common during rainy weather. In dry climates, lack of moisture can produce a black tip, but this is strictly cosmetic and won't affect taste.

## Harvest it

To encourage the growth of a strong and healthy root system, don't harvest your perennial artichokes the first year. Leave them to bloom. During their second year, cut off the artichoke heads before the scales begin to open, leaving about three inches of stem attached to the bud. Once you cut off the central bud in the middle, side shoots with smaller, more tender buds will emerge. You'll be able to harvest the side shoots as they grow, reaping an extended harvest. If you grow an annual variety like Imperial Star, harvest the buds before the first frost.

**Store:** Leave a stalk attached to the head and put it in a container of water in the refrigerator. Change the water daily. For the best flavor, aim to eat your artichoke within a week.

**Preserve:** Freeze artichokes by first blanching them with lemon in boiling water. Once they turn bright green, remove them from the heat. Let them dry fully and then freeze. Eat the artichokes within eight months to enjoy the best flavor.

# Grilled Marinated Artichoke

Artichokes can seem like an indulgence, maybe because they're dipped in butter and savored leaf by leaf when eaten as an appetizer. Another way to enjoy your artichokes is to marinate and grill them. They make a rich addition to salads and pasta. Serves 4.

## Ingredients:

2 artichokes

1 lemon, cut in wedges

*Marinade:*

¼ cup olive oil

¼ cup lemon juice

3 sprigs thyme

3 sprigs oregano

3 garlic cloves, sliced

1 tsp black pepper

½ tsp kosher salt

Pinch of red pepper flakes

## Preparation:

1. Boil artichokes with lemon wedges for 30 minutes or until fork tender.

2. Mix all marinade ingredients in a bowl.

3. Drain artichokes and cool, cut into quarters, and put in bowl with the marinade. Make sure the artichokes are well covered.

4. Let sit for 4 hours, or preferably overnight.

5. Grill until the artichokes have grill marks. Serve warm.

# ASPARAGUS

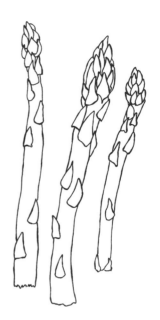

**High in vitamins C and K, asparagus can** be baked, boiled, grilled, or sautéed and still retain its intense flavor. But the most amazing thing about asparagus may be that while it takes time to become established, it can live for 30 to 50 years.

**Varieties:** Most of the asparagus spears you see in grocery stores come from Jersey varieties, including Jersey Knight, Jersey King, Jersey Giant, and Jersey Supreme. Jersey varieties are sturdy because they're male plants, which means they devote all their energy to producing spears instead of seeds. Waltham Washington and Mary Washington varieties are also hardy, rust-resistant types frequently found in gardens. If you live in a warm climate, consider the Princeville variety, which does well in the heat. Purple Passion is a gorgeous purple heirloom variety, until it's cooked and loses much of its color.

**Companion plants:** Companion plants don't work well with asparagus, which requires a lot of nutrients. Weeds and companion plants can siphon away those nutrients. Also, after harvesting, the asparagus plant grows huge and can easily swamp everything around it. In short, it's best to keep your asparagus separate.

# Where it thrives

**Regional compatibility:** Asparagus can be grown almost anywhere across the contiguous United States. It does best, however, in northern climates where it gets a period of rest, or dormancy, during the winter. After a cold winter, the warmth of spring jolts asparagus to life. If it's not allowed to regularly go dormant, asparagus can wear out and die. Asparagus also has a harder time getting established in southern regions where summers are long, hot, and humid.

**Optimal sun and shade:** Asparagus has a lot of surface area in its foliage and loves to bask in the warm sun. So choose a sunny spot for your plants. They can tolerate partial shade, but plants grown in full sun are more resilient.

**Soil type:** Asparagus grows best in sandy soil that's heavily composted, but does just fine in most garden soil. It will lose some of its vigor in highly acidic soil. Walk around your asparagus patch in winter and spring; asparagus spears like soil that is well-aerated, not hard packed.

**Resilience:** While it takes a few years to become established, asparagus can eventually sustain itself through dry conditions and even drought. More tolerant of salt than most perennials, asparagus also grows well in coastal areas. It can survive short periods of flooding but prolonged soggy soils will rot the shallow crowns. In hot dry regions, young plants need a good supply of water and fertilizer.

# Planting

**Best time of year to plant:** Plant your crowns in the early spring when the soil is no longer frozen or mucky. In especially warm regions, asparagus can be planted in the late fall or winter.

**From seeds:** Growing from seed is generally harder than growing from crowns. If you choose to grow from seed, it's best to start indoors 12 to 14 weeks before the first spring frost. Plant seeds one-half to three-quarter inches deep in two-inch pots. Transplant your seedlings outside when daytime temperatures have reached the 70s.

**From cuttings:** Crowns are year-old root sections you can buy from a seed catalogue. This is the most reliable way to establish your asparagus patch. Plant them as soon as the soil thaws in the spring. Asparagus crowns and transplants must be planted in trenches.

Here's how to prepare your soil for asparagus:

1. Dig a trench 12 inches deep. Take the excavated soil and mix it with compost in a wheelbarrow. I like to dig my trenches so that if you looked at a cross section, you'd see a W. I place the crown in the middle of the W, or the raised soil in the middle of the trench, to ensure better drainage. Planting this way also lets the roots spread out on either side, pointed downward, allowing the plant to take hold more quickly.

2. Fill in the trench with four inches of the soil/compost mixture so the trench is now eight inches deep. If you're planting in heavy clay soil, pile in eight inches of compost/soil mixture so you have a four-inch trench left.

3. Place the crowns in the trench about 12 inches apart. Be sure to separate and untangle the roots. Asparagus planted too close together will produce spindly, thin shoots that may not be strong enough to push through to the surface.

4. Cover the crowns with four to six inches of soil. If you're transplanting seedlings, cover them with soil halfway up the stem. As the asparagus spears begin to emerge, continue to keep the shoots covered. Fill in the trenches with any extra soil and compost mix until the entire trench

is level with the rest of the bed. This preparation should sustain your plants through the first growing season.

## Growing

Asparagus roots grow horizontally, not vertically, which means your asparagus will eventually have a fairly dense, thick mat of intertwined roots. In early spring, young shoots will pierce the soil and, if left unpicked, turn into tall, fern-like plants. Apply a layer of mulch or straw after harvesting and before winter to insulate the roots. In the spring, new spears will grow through the mulch and be much stronger for it.

**Weeding:** Weed your asparagus. Nearby plants can siphon off nutrients and keep your delicious asparagus from getting established. When pulling weeds, try not to disturb the shallow roots. If they're annual weeds, cut them at the base rather than pulling them out. If your weeds are deep-rooted perennials, you'll just have to yank them or risk losing your patch.

**Watering:** When young, asparagus needs heavy, consistent watering. Keep beds moist but never soggy to reduce the risk of disease. Established asparagus will do just fine with less water. In areas of the country that get regular bursts of rain, you won't need to do additional watering.

**Fertilizing after planting:** Each spring, add one to two inches of compost before the spears push through the soil. In addition to compost, use a balanced fertilizer for newly planted crowns—one with equal amounts of nitrogen, phosphorus, and potassium, like a 10-10-10 or 15-15-15 blend. If the leaves look yellow or weak, consider adding a fertilizer with high nitrogen, like a 10-5-5 blend, but don't overdo it. Nitrogen loading produces plants with too much foliage and weak roots.

# Challenges

As you've probably gathered, there's a lot of waiting involved in growing asparagus. Be patient and try not get too frustrated with this late bloomer. Your patience will be rewarded with many years of fruitful harvests. On the other hand, asparagus can easily overrun the rest of your garden if you don't keep it in check. It spreads through rhizomes, a horizontal underground stem that produces new shoots each growing season.

**Pests:** Asparagus plants don't attract many pests. Their one major foe is the asparagus beetle, which is about one-third of an inch long and can be picked off by hand. Get rid of these bugs when it's too cold for them to fly, typically in early morning and evening. Removing plant debris in the winter helps keep beetles at bay because that's where they hide and develop.

**Diseases:** Purple spot, rust, and root rot are soil-borne fungal diseases that can plague asparagus plants. Overwatering and moist growing conditions increase the likelihood of disease. If you have to plant a patch in less than ideal conditions, consider buying crowns, which are more rot-resistant.

# Harvest it

Asparagus is ready to harvest after it has grown spears thicker than a pencil. This usually happens in the third year. Take a sharp knife to the spears when they are six to eight inches long but before they flower, or they'll be too tough to eat. Cut them just below the surface of the soil. Be careful not to slice into any newly emerging spears and try not to pull up the roots. Leave a handful of spears unpicked. The delicate fern-like foliage gives roots energy during the growing season so plants can keep pumping out delicious spears each spring.

**Store:** Asparagus deteriorates pretty quickly after harvesting, so pick it just before cooking. It can be refrigerated for up to a week.

**Preserve:** Asparagus freezes well. Before popping the spears in the freezer, blanch them to prevent freezer burn. To blanch, boil washed spears for two or three minutes and let them dry thoroughly.

## Balsamic and Honey Roasted Asparagus

Adding a touch of sweetness to balsamic vinegar creates a delightful burst of flavor, and is especially good when drizzled on a sturdy vegetable like asparagus. Serve this easy side dish with pasta or as part of a hearty winter meal. Serves 6.

### Ingredients:

2 lbs asparagus spears

2 T olive oil

Salt and pepper

1 tsp dried rosemary or thyme

3 T balsamic vinegar

1 T honey (or maple syrup)

### Preparation:

1. Preheat oven to 400 degrees.

2. Spread asparagus on a rimmed baking sheet. Drizzle with olive oil, then sprinkle with salt, pepper, and dried herb. Roast for 18-20 minutes.

3. Whisk vinegar and honey, then drizzle over the spears and serve.

# BEANS

**Most beans are garden annuals,** but a few can be grown as perennials and will produce a prolific harvest each season. Perennial beans are high in protein. They also have a much appreciated superpower shared by all legumes: they can improve your soil's fertility by adding nitrogen.

**Varieties:** Perennial beans come in two main varieties. Scarlet Runner Beans are well suited to temperate regions and yield beautiful purple and black beans encapsulated in vibrant green pods. Hummingbirds love this plant's bright red flowers. The Asian Winged Bean is a warm-weather plant that is less resilient but also beautiful. Each square pod has a fringed wing, and the soft purple flowers attract bees, hummingbirds, and other pollinators.

**Companion plants:** Beans make a great companion to most crops because of their nitrogen-fixing powers. They'll do well if you plant them alongside marigolds, which can help repel the Mexican bean beetle. Do not plant your beans next to onions and garlic, which can prevent bean seeds from germinating.

# Where it thrives

**Regional compatibility:** Scarlet Runner Beans are native to North America and thrive in climates where temperatures stay above 10 degrees. Winged Beans hail from Asia and love tropical heat, so they're sensitive to frost and are typically grown in this country as annuals.

**Optimal sun and shade:** To be productive, beans require full sun for more than six hours a day.

**Soil type:** Beans like a well-drained, warm soil that is light or sandy. They do not grow well in acidic soils. If your soil has low pH, you might need to add lime.

**Resilience:** Winged Beans are prolific growers in warm areas but don't do as well in the cold. They easily succumb to frost, droughts, and flooding. Scarlet Runner Beans, on the other hand, grow well in most places.

# Planting

**Best time of year to plant:** Plant your perennial beans in late spring, unless you live in a warm, frost-free zone. Then plant in the fall for a winter harvest.

**From seeds:** Beans like warm soil and have a hard time germinating when it's cold and damp. Give your beans a head start by starting them indoors three weeks before the last frost. Plant them in four-inch pots to give the roots room to grow and expand. Two weeks after the first two leaves develop, move them outside. Even better, sow bean seeds directly into the ground to avoid the stress of transplanting. Bean roots are particularly sensitive to being disturbed. Wait until daytime temperatures reach the mid-60s and plant seeds two inches apart, roughly one inch deep.

# Growing

Once beans sprout, they're quick to grow. If you start them inside, make sure not to leave your seedlings in the pot for long or they'll become leggy and weak. Beans grow best when they have the support of a trellis or fence. It's pretty easy to train them to climb because the tendrils are always searching for something to grab onto. Bean plants can grow to over eight feet tall. If you're worried about planting your tropical Winged Beans where it's warm enough, plant them near a patio, house, or a retaining wall that can absorb heat during the day and release it at night. Use mulch to keep weeds in check and conserve water during dry spells.

**Weeding:** Beans grow fast and tall, so weeds aren't much of a problem. But a good reason to keep beans weed-free is so slugs can't hide in them during the day and come out at night to feed on the plant's low-hanging leaves.

**Watering:** Beans need a lot of water when they start to producing flowers and pods, and can suck up about a half-inch a day. During hot summer weather, you may have to water your beans daily once they start blooming.

**Fertilizing after planting:** Beans are nitrogen fixers, meaning they take care of their own nitrogen needs. As the leaves take nitrogen out of the air, little nodules on the roots put it into the soil, where the plant can draw on it. If you decide to fertilize your beans, use a fertilizer high in phosphorus like guano or bone meal, and feed your plants with potassium by adding kelp meal. Don't give it more nitrogen or your beans may grow more leaves than beans.

# Challenges

Scarlet Runner Beans are a cinch to grow, but Winged Beans can be tricky. These tropical plants flower only in places that get fewer than 12 hours of daylight. This makes them hard to grow in most of the United States, where peak summer days run at least 12 hours.

**Pests:** The leaves are more vulnerable to bugs than the pods. Leafhoppers are tiny, lime-green pests that won't kill plants but do stress them out, making them susceptible to disease and other pests. Signs you may have a hopper problem are curling leaves. Shake the vine to see if adult leafhoppers start hopping about. If you have an infestation spray the plant periodically with an insecticidal soap.

Mexican bean beetles are also a threat. Look for copper-colored, hard-shelled insects that eat entire leaves, leaving only the veins. Keep them under control by picking off these pesky beetles when you see them. Aphids like to feed on bean leaves too, and while *they* won't kill your plants, they can transmit a mosaic virus that will. Snip off the affected areas and spray plants with an insecticidal soap.

**Diseases:** While beans might be a little finicky, they don't have many disease problems, making them a nearly carefree perennial.

# Harvest it

Once beans start forming, pick them as often as possible to increase yields. If you want slender and tender beans, pick them every three to five days. For dry beans, just leave them on the vine to dry out. Bean flowers are edible so toss them in a summer salad or use them as a garnish.

**Store:** Cook with beans the day you pick them because that's when they taste best. If you do store them, wrap them in a damp paper towel and plastic bag. You can refrigerate your beans for up to a week.

**Preserve:** Storage beans, or dried beans, are the ones you left on the vine to dry. These beans can be shelled and stored in an airtight container. Soak them overnight before cooking.

## Bean Ragout

Use your favorite perennial bean for this simple ragout. Reminiscent of a tomato-laden stew, Bean Ragout makes a hearty vegetarian dish. Serve with a braised green and a grain, or over pasta. Serves 4 as a side dish, 2 as the main course.

### Ingredients:

2 T olive oil

4 cloves garlic, minced or chopped

½ medium white onion, chopped

Red wine (optional)

1 T + 1 tsp tomato paste

1 ½ - 1 ¾ cups cooked beans

1 15-ounce can of diced tomatoes or fresh diced tomatoes

1 T fresh oregano, chopped

1 T fresh thyme, chopped

Salt and pepper

### Preparation:

1. Heat olive oil over medium heat and add garlic. Let cook for 1 minute, then add onion. Cook for about 5 minutes, stirring constantly until onions are translucent and aromatic.

2. Add a splash or two of red wine and cook down, then stir in tomato paste.

3. Add the beans and tomatoes, and a pinch each of salt and pepper.

4. Cook until the beans and tomatoes are heated through, then add the fresh herbs and salt and pepper to taste.

# BROCCOLI

**Perennial broccoli is versatile, easy to cook, and an impressive** source of calcium, iron, fiber, and B vitamins. This plant loves cool temperatures, which makes it an especially good fit for cold-weather gardeners.

**Varieties:** Most varieties of broccoli grow as annuals, producing a large head at the end of the season and that's that. But perennial broccoli, also known as sprouting broccoli, produces many small, tender florets. Broccoli can be grown as a perennial even in areas where temperatures hit minus 20 degrees. The most popular variety is Nine Star, which produces an abundance of white florets. Gailan, or Chinese Broccoli, yields many small and tender florets with smooth stems that are delicious. Leaf broccoli varieties have leaves with a sweet kale-like flavor. Another popular variety is Broccoli Raab, which tends to be a little bitter.

**Companion plants:** Plant broccoli with light feeders that won't compete for nutrients like beets, potatoes, onions, carrots, Swiss chard, or peas. This perennial also does well with aromatic herbs, like dill and rosemary, that help repel insects.

# Where it thrives

**Regional compatibility:** Broccoli can grow all across the United States but does best where summer temperatures don't exceed 80 degrees. When heat stressed, broccoli tends to bolt, or flower prematurely, and isn't able to grow tasty florets. To prevent against bolting, shade the soil with mulch as the summer heats up.

**Optimal sun and shade:** This vegetable thrives when it gets about six hours of sunlight a day. In hotter climates, it benefits from afternoon shade.

**Soil type:** Broccoli does best in well-drained, heavily composted, sandy soil. Because of its shallow root structure, it can be grown in soil that's not very deep.

**Resilience:** Broccoli adapts well to cold temperatures and mild frost. Dry conditions aren't a problem either if the soil is kept rich, well-nourished, and cooled with compost and mulch. Prolonged heat, on the other hand, can stress broccoli and turn florets bitter.

# Planting

**Best time of year to plant:** Excessive heat will produce spindly and unproductive plants, so plant broccoli during your cool season. This may mean winter in Florida and California, or spring or fall in New Hampshire and Montana. Cool temperatures drive up sugar levels and the soil stays moist, producing healthier, more flavorful florets.

**From seeds:** Plant two to three broccoli seeds about a half-inch deep in four-inch pots. No heat mat is needed for starting broccoli seeds. In fact, this vegetable can germinate in soil temperatures as low as 40 degrees. After the plants have sprouted three leaves, transplant only the strongest-looking plants into the garden, spacing them one to two feet apart. Get the seedlings in the ground before they become root bound. Plants left in small pots for too long will bolt as soon as they're transplanted.

If you wish to plant directly in your garden, sow three to four broccoli seeds a foot, about a half-inch deep. Thin to one plant every two feet once the seeds have sprouted. The farther apart you plant your broccoli, the more likely the florets will grow.

## Growing

Broccoli has shallow roots, so be careful not to disturb them when planting companion vegetables and herbs. For that reason, don't pull up the roots of any annuals planted around the broccoli when cleaning up in the fall. Simply cut them at the base of the stem and leave the soil, and its community of organisms, undisturbed. Broccoli can easily become top heavy. To stabilize it, tie it to stakes. I place two bamboo poles in an X on either side of the plant to form a brace. This way, the plants have something to lean on. Once broccoli topples over, it usually doesn't recover. Broccoli plants don't need to be pruned, but do remove any wilted bottom leaves to prevent mildew.

**Weeding:** Weeds tend to be a concern only when broccoli first sprouts. After the plant starts to take off, it's generally hard for weeds to grow underneath because the leaf canopy is so large.

**Watering:** Give your broccoli plenty of water. A lack of water can prevent broccoli from developing its signature florets. Aim to give your plants roughly one to two inches of water each week. Let the soil dry out between waterings so the roots don't rot.

**Fertilizing after planting:** If you notice yellowing leaves or plants that aren't standing up straight, add a nitrogen-rich fertilizer like blood meal. It is almost impossible to overfeed broccoli.

# Challenges

Heat stress is broccoli's biggest challenge, which explains why so many gardeners plant it in the fall. I recommend testing a few varieties to see what grows best in your area.

**Pests:** Cutworms, cabbage worms, and flea beetles are all broccoli pests. You can protect it from cutworms by placing a cardboard paper towel tube over the broccoli stalk while it's young and thin. Another way to ward off cutworms, and slugs too, is to ring the stem with diatomaceous earth (DE). Cabbage worms can be picked off by hand or controlled using an insecticidal soap.

Flea beetles are much harder to control. They're fast moving with a hard shell that protects them from many organic treatments. They do not like wet leaves, so misting your plants can keep the numbers down. But the best defense is to place yellow sticky traps every five feet around your plants. The beetles are attracted to the yellow tape, and their small bodies are no match for the adhesive. You can also protect your plants by covering them with a floating row cover. One reason I prefer planting broccoli in the fall is that flea beetles are less active once nighttime temperatures have cooled.

**Diseases:** Club root fungus and various types of rot can attack broccoli. To prevent this from happening, keep soil well-drained. If your plant is hit by club root, increasing the soil pH by adding some lime can slow the infection. But ultimately you'll have to remove infected plants and avoid planting any new broccoli in that spot.

Yellow patches on leaves, a symptom of downy mildew, are usually caused by moist weather. Keep leaves as dry as possible and don't crowd the plants so air can circulate around them freely.

# Harvest it

If you want your broccoli to sprout continuously, harvest the florets before they flower and produce seeds. Cut off the florets with a sharp knife. If your plant does bolt, use the slightly spicy flowers as a garnish or a peppery addition to salads.

**Store:** Wrap your broccoli loosely in a damp paper towel and refrigerate for up to three days. Or chill it with stems submerged in ice water, and the head covered with a plastic bag, for up to a week. Don't wash before refrigerating or store it in a sealed container because this can make it moldy.

**Preserve:** Broccoli can be frozen but first blanch, or boil it, for two minutes. I like to dice my vegetables before blanching and freezing them so I can add the chunks to a hot pan without needing to defrost the florets first.

# Savory Broccoli Galette

A savory pie without the fuss, a galette can be thrown together with whatever vegetables, cheeses, or spreads you have on hand. In this recipe, the crunch of broccoli is set off by the softness of the dough. Pair with a salad and you've got dinner. Serves 4 as a main course.

## Ingredients:

Your favorite pie dough, chilled

*Filling:*

1 pound broccoli

1 ½ T olive oil

Salt and pepper

½ cup Ricotta cheese or vegan cheese

Egg or cream wash (or vegan substitute)

*Topping:*

Red pepper flakes

Parmesan cheese

## Preparation:

**Dough:**

Roll out dough to make a circle with a 12-inch diameter. Transfer dough to a parchment-lined baking sheet.

**Filling and baking:**

1. Chop broccoli in 3-inch pieces and drizzle with oil. Add salt and pepper. Roast at 375 degrees for 15 minutes.

2. Spread cheese on the rolled out dough, leaving about 2 inches of space around the edges. Add roasted broccoli.

3. Fold the edges of the galette so it partially covers the broccoli, leaving the middle open. It doesn't have to look perfect.

4. Brush the top of dough with an egg or cream wash.

5. Bake in 400 degree oven for 30 to 40 minutes, until the crust is nicely brown.

6. Sprinkle with red pepper flakes and Parmesan. Serve warm.

# GARLIC

**Garlic is winter hardy, grows easily, and takes** up very little space in a garden. An ancient bulbous vegetable, it grows from a single clove that multiplies in the ground. Most people grow it as an annual, but if you harvest only the big plants and leave behind the small ones, you'll have a perennial garlic bed that regrows every year. Close relatives include onions, shallots, and leeks.

**Varieties:** Garlic comes in two varieties. Softneck, which includes Artichoke and Silverskins, does best in warmer climates. For cold climates, go with a hardneck variety like Rocambole, Purple Stripe, or Porcelain.

**Companion plants:** Garlic is a wonderful companion plant for many of your favorite garden annuals. Plant a border of it to ward off hungry deer and rabbits. Its pungent odor deters pests, including cabbage worms, spider mites, aphids, carrot rust flies, and Japanese beetles. This makes it a good neighbor to beets, celery, carrots, tomatoes, and cabbage. But the chemicals that make garlic a powerful pest deterrent can also inhibit the growth of peas, beans, and asparagus, so keep it separate from these crops.

## Where it thrives

**Regional compatibility:** Garlic is resistant to frost and even a hard freeze if the soil is well-drained. Most varieties actually prefer a cold climate. But if you have soggy soil, cold temperatures will freeze the water and displace newly planted garlic cloves, causing them to rot as the soil warms in the spring.

**Optimal sun and shade:** Garlic grows best in full sun.

**Soil type:** Ideally, plant garlic in loose, well-drained soil that's high in organic matter. Loose soil prevents the bulb from becoming misshapen as it develops.

**Resilience:** You have only to visit my garlic bed in late winter to see proof of garlic's cold hardiness as its green tips poke through the snow. But the plants still need protection. I apply a layer of mulch to help the crop weather long, cold winters. Garlic grows well in light, sandy soil but needs to be watered frequently during dry spells to promote healthy root development. Once garlic is established, it can tolerate drought.

## Planting

**Best time of year to plant:** Garlic can be planted in the spring, but fall is the best time because the plants are more likely to yield large bulbs with intense flavor. Make sure to plant it before the ground freezes.

**From seeds:** Garlic is not typically grown from true seed. In fact, seed companies traditionally sell only cloves.

**From cuttings:** The easiest way to grow garlic is from the same cloves you enjoy in the kitchen. Separate the bulb into individual cloves two to three days before planting. Keep the papery wrapping on each clove to prevent it from rotting. Plant cloves four inches deep and about six inches apart, with the pointy side facing up. Apply mulch to protect against the winter chill. Garlic needs roughly 6 to 12 weeks of cold temperatures to develop harvestable bulbs. If you're planting garlic in a warm, frost-free climate, chill the cloves before planting by storing them in the fridge for up to 12 weeks.

## Growing

Cover your plants with a generous layer of mulch in the fall. The colder the winter, the more mulch you should pile on. Many gardeners choose to keep mulch in place after spring to limit weed growth. For Hardneck varieties, you'll notice a round, leafless flower stem emerging from the center of the leaves about three weeks before harvest. This is the scape. Some growers cut off scapes to produce a more robust bulb. If left uncut, garlic scapes will bloom into pretty, whitish-pink pom-poms that bees love.

**Weeding:** Weed your garlic plants regularly. Mulching helps keep the weeds at bay.

**Watering:** Water your garlic every three to five days in spring when the bulb is forming. But don't water it after July or the bulbs may rot. In fact, you might want to harvest your garlic early if you're experiencing a lot of rain. One rainy summer I gently tugged a stalk and found a moldy, mushy bulb barely clinging to it. Not surprisingly, the entire patch was rotten.

Fall weather is usually wet enough to support healthy roots until winter sets in. But if you've got a hot, dry fall, soaking your garlic once every 10 days and letting the soil dry between waterings will encourage deep root growth. If you're growing garlic in a place with relatively warm winters, water your plants occasionally over the winter.

**Fertilizing after planting:** In the spring, when your plants are about a foot tall, boost growth by shaking on a high-nitrogen fertilizer, like blood meal, especially if you notice yellowing leaves. Stop fertilizing once the garlic scape appears—you want your plants' energy to go toward developing bulbs, not leaves. Avoid using fertilizer high in nitrogen during a fall planting because it encourages leaf growth instead of the root development necessary for the plant to get through winter.

## Challenges

Knowing when to harvest may be your biggest challenge in growing garlic. Harvest too soon and the bulbs won't mature. Harvest too late and the bulbs may already have begun to open. In neither case will the bulbs store well.

**Pests:** Pests are not a problem because this herb repels them.

**Diseases:** Garlic is susceptible to white rot, a fungus that attacks roots and leaves in the winter. It's also vulnerable to garlic rust, a fungal disease that attacks the leaves. To prevent rot and rust from spreading, dig out all the infected plants after harvesting. Do not compost the infected leaves or roots. Instead, burn the infected plant material, bring it to your local green waste drop-off, or otherwise get it off your property.

## Harvest it

You know it's time to pick garlic when the bottom two leaves yellow and wither. This typically occurs in July or August. Expect a later harvest date if you plant in the spring. If you want green garlic, harvest it in May and June when the stalks are young and tender. To harvest garlic, carefully loosen the soil and dig out the bulbs, taking care not to tear the paper skin. This thin covering protects garlic from going bad. You can also harvest the garlic scape once it curls. Scapes appear only once a season, so don't miss out. They're delicious sauteed in oil and salted.

To keep your garlic patch going year after year, leave a few bulbs in the soil and lay down some mulch. The following spring, new garlic will push through the soil on its own. If you harvest all the bulbs, you'll have to plant new ones each fall or spring to keep the harvest going.

**Store:** Keep fresh garlic at room temperature in a container that breathes, like a plastic bag with holes in it, a wire or mesh basket, or a paper bag. Do not store garlic in the refrigerator or it will sprout. You can eat sprouted garlic, but once a green shoot pops out of the clove, the bulb's more likely to turn into mush. Scapes, on the other hand, store well in a sealed bag in the fridge.

**Preserve:** For long-term storage, hang or place garlic bulbs in a dark, dry, warm spot for a couple of weeks. Once the bulbs are dry, or cured, store them with the wrappers still on. Garlic flavor increases when the bulbs are dried. You can freeze scapes in a sealed bag for up to a year. I love to make scape pesto and freeze it in ice cube trays. When it's pasta night, I take out a few cubes and throw them in a pot of rinsed pasta. After they melt, I shake on a little Parmesan cheese.

# Roasted Garlic Spread

Roasting garlic mellows out the sharp bite while deepening the flavor. This spread is delicious served on bread, or in sauces. You can stir in Dijon mustard or olive oil, or mix the spread into a cream-based dip. Makes ½ cup.

## Ingredients:

4 heads of garlic

Olive oil for drizzling

¼ tsp salt

⅛ tsp pepper

## Preparation:

1. Preheat the oven to 400 degrees.

2. Cut the tops off of each garlic head so the cloves are exposed. Drizzle each with enough olive oil so that it runs down into the cloves (about 1 tsp per head).

3. Wrap in foil and roast in the oven for 50 minutes.

4. When the garlic heads are done, the insides should be soft. Squeeze out the garlic from the cloves and mash with a fork. Add salt and pepper.

# PEPPER

**Peppers are sweet or hot, big or small. There's** a pepper for everyone. Much like tomatoes, peppers are true perennials only in frost-free climates. With a little extra care and attention, they can be grown indoors through the winter. Given enough sunlight, peppers can also be picked throughout the year.

**Varieties:** Bell Peppers are the most common sweet pepper. Other sweet staples include Cornitos and Sprinter. For a twist on the traditional, check out Oda, a brilliant purple pepper with stark white flesh. A sweet cherry pepper called Red Cheese Pepper makes a great snack. Cubanelle Peppers are long, thin, and look like they should be hot, but they're not. Italian frying peppers like Jimmy Nordello are best cooked in olive oil but taste great raw as well. If sweet isn't your thing, try hot peppers, like Jalapenos, Chipotle or, if you dare, Ghost Peppers. Spicy peppers heat up even more in warm climates, are easier to grow than Bell Peppers, and thrive almost anywhere. As with every pepper, they cannot survive cold winters unless brought inside.

**Companion plants:** Peppers and basil grow well together because they thrive in the same growing conditions. Peppers also benefit from growing among taller plants, like okra, which provide a natural windbreak for these brittle plants.

# Where it thrives

**Regional compatibility:** Peppers need a long warm season to mature, so they're best grown in southern regions. In northern climates, it's a race against the weather since peppers tend to ripen in late September. Start seeds or cuttings inside on a heat mat to give peppers a chance to ripen before it gets cold.

**Optimal sun and shade:** Peppers love the heat of the sun, so plant them where they'll get six to eight hours of it a day.

**Soil type:** Sandy, loose soils packed with compost work well. Peppers can tolerate slightly acidic soil.

**Resilience:** Peppers are heat-loving plants and, once established, adapt well to drought. They can't tolerate frost, which kills them.

# Planting

**Best time of year to plant:** Start seedlings indoors in the spring.

**From seeds:** Pepper seeds won't germinate in cold soil, so sow seeds about a quarter-inch deep in planting pots or flats and keep them warm on a heat mat. When three true leaves appear, transplant the seedlings into larger pots. Move them into your garden after the last frost. To ease the transition, set out your plants on warm spring days and move them back inside during cool nights. This process, known as hardening off, prevents your peppers from being shocked when you finally plant them outside. Plant seedlings 12 to 18 inches apart and, if you want to be extra cautious, protect them against the chill by draping them with a row cover.

**From cuttings:** Pepper is best grown from seed.

# Growing

Peppers have fairly shallow root systems and do best with some kind of structural support. I've tied peppers to sticks, bamboo stakes, and tomato cages to keep them from falling over and breaking. In very high heat, peppers drop their flowers, which leaves you with fewer peppers at the end of the season. To keep soil moist and weeds to a minimum, use plenty of mulch.

**Weeding:** Keep your plants free of weeds to limit pests.

**Watering:** Peppers need about an inch of water a week. Make sure to water them from the time they flower until the peppers ripen because thirsty plants will drop fruit and wilt. But don't overdo it. Overwatered plants can drop leaves and bear discolored fruit.

**Fertilizing:** Peppers need phosphorus and calcium to grow big, blemish-free fruits, so add bone meal to replenish the soil when you see the first flower bud.

# Challenges

Peppers can easily fall victim to a host of fungal diseases. Take care to water the soil and not the leaves.

**Pests:** The pepper maggot is a formidable foe of organic peppers. These pests spend their lives inside fruits after the adult flies lay their eggs. Once hatched, the maggots eat out the inside of the pepper, making it rot prematurely. Pepper maggots are hard to control. However, adults are attracted to the color yellow, so one option is to hang yellow sticky traps from late May to early June. Pepper maggot flies also prefer sweet peppers, so I plant a border of decoy hot peppers to attract the flies.

Caterpillars and cutworms like to seek shade under pepper plants. You can spray these pests with Bt, a natural soil bacteria, or spread a thin layer of diatomaceous earth (DE) at the base of plants. Peppers are also attacked by aphids that hang out near developing flower buds. Spraying the bugs with insecticidal soap should take care of them.

**Diseases:** Blight is a fungal disease that can affect both young and mature plants. There's little you can do about blight once plants have it, but removing infected leaves can at least prevent the disease from invading the stems. Be careful not to compost the infected leaves so it doesn't spread.

Blossom end rot occurs when there's either a deficiency of calcium in the soil or large variations in soil moisture. Black and brown leathery patches appear at the blossom end of fruits. Infected fruit is still delicious—just cut out the brown spots.

## Harvest it

All peppers start off green and change color as they ripen. You can harvest them while green, but if you wait for the color change you'll have a more flavorful pepper. This is certainly the way to go if you're like me and eat your peppers like an apple. Use scissors to harvest your crop instead of tearing off the peppers by hand, because pepper branches are brittle and easily rip away from the plant.

**Store:** Whole peppers keep their flavor and texture best when stored at room temperature. They'll keep for up to a week. Refrigerate cut peppers to keep them fresh for up to two weeks.

**Preserve:** You can freeze raw or roasted peppers for up to 10 months.

# Stuffed Bell Peppers with Tahini Yogurt Dressing

The bell pepper serves as an edible bowl, adding a zestiness and crunch to this salad. Creamy tahini yogurt dressing helps create a seamless dish. If you don't have tahini on hand, use almond butter, or add fresh herbs for a green goddess-like dressing. Serves 4.

## Ingredients:

4 cups couscous salad (see page 77)

4 bell peppers

Olive oil

*For the dressing:*

¼ cup tahini

2 T olive oil

2 cloves garlic, pressed

½ cup greek yogurt or non-dairy yogurt

2 T lemon juice

2 T honey or agave

½ cup water

¼ - ½ tsp salt

¼ - ½ tsp pepper

## Preparation:

1. Preheat oven to 400 degrees. Cut off tops of peppers and gut the insides to remove the seeds. Fill each with 1 cup of couscous salad (or until filled). Place in an 8x8 baking dish with 1 inch of water, then drizzle on olive oil. Bake for 40 minutes and serve hot.

2. While the peppers are baking, make the dressing. In a small bowl, stir together tahini, olive oil, and garlic. Add yogurt, lemon juice, and honey. Whisk in water, salt, and pepper. For a thinner sauce, add more water 1 table-spoon at a time. Drizzle over peppers or serve on the side.

# RADICCHIO

**Radicchio is a bright purple-red,** cool weather-loving perennial. Like cabbage, it grows heads that can be chopped up and thrown in a salad or cooked into pastas, omelettes, and more. The bitter flavor adds character to dishes. This perennial is so resilient, it grows in the cracks between stone pavers.

**Varieties:** The most commonly planted variety is Radicchio di Verona, also known as Radicchio Rosso, which grows a cabbage-like head. For longer, spear-shaped radicchio, opt for Radicchio di Treviso. For radicchio connoisseurs, nontraditional varieties include Chioggia and Castelfranco.

**Companion plants:** I like to grow my radicchio at the base of taller perennials so they can enjoy some afternoon shade and avoid getting heat stressed.

# Where it thrives

**Regional compatibility:** Radicchio can grow almost anywhere in the United States, though it prefers temperate weather. Its seeds won't germinate when temperatures climb higher than the mid-70s so plant it in spring or fall. In hotter regions, winter is the optimal growing season. Even when it's cold enough to freeze over, radicchio can be thawed and eaten.

**Optimal sun and shade:** In cool-weather areas, plant radicchio in full sunshine. In warmer weather, give your radicchio partial shade.

**Soil type:** Radicchio tastes best when grown in loamy, well-drained soil, but this vegetable isn't picky. Years after planting it one spring, I found it growing in neglected corners of the greenhouse and in tiny cracks in the pavement—basically anywhere the roots could take hold.

**Resilience:** Radicchio is most susceptible to weather extremes when young. As it matures, the plant is better able to withstand cold and frost. In extreme heat or drought, it needs lots of moisture and mulching to taste good and do well. The more drought and heat stressed radicchio is, the more bitter it tastes.

# Planting

**Best time of year to plant:** Plant radicchio in the spring or fall if you live where temperatures are moderate. If you live in a hot climate, plant in early spring or late fall so it doesn't get heat stressed. Plant it in midsummer if you live in a very cold part of the country where nighttime temperatures rarely climb higher than 55 degrees.

**From seeds:** Start seeds in late spring, about three to four weeks before your last frost. Seeds are best sown in cool temperatures. If you wait too long and the soil warms to over 60 degrees, radicchio seeds won't germinate. If you're planting in pots, keep them outside in a sheltered area so they sprout. Plant two seeds in a two-inch pot about one-quarter inch deep. Thin to the healthiest seedling once plants have sprouted three leaves. Once seedlings are three inches tall, transplant them into the garden about eight inches apart. Don't worry about a late spring frost because these plants can weather cold snaps.

If you'd rather skip the containers and plant directly in the garden, sow a few seeds in every foot of soil before the temperature climbs above 70 degrees. Keep newly planted areas moist until all the seeds have sprouted. After your plants grow to be about five inches tall, thin them by snipping seedlings at the base rather than digging them out, so you're left with plants 8 to 12 inches apart. Don't fret about the spacing; over the years these plants will bunch together.

**From cuttings:** Radicchio is always grown from seed, but you can expect it to regrow after cutting off the leaves.

## Growing

Like cabbage, radicchio has a shallow root system. It needs mulch, and you can just use the crowns and leaves left over from old plants. Mulching helps protect the roots from being disturbed and conserves moisture, which makes the radicchio taste better. During the heat of summer, radicchio does best in afternoon shade. Too much heat stress will cause it to bolt, or flower early.

**Weeding:** Radicchio is a short plant that can easily be shaded by taller weeds, so keep your beds cleared.

**Watering:** This moisture-loving plant prefers one to two inches of water a week. Once the head starts to form, and about two weeks before harvest, give it about three inches a week to keep the leaves from becoming too bitter.

**Fertilizing after planting:** Since radicchio has a shallow root system, it needs every bit of organic matter it can get, so feed it a healthy dose of compost every spring. No additional fertilizer is necessary. In fact, excessive nitrogen will just increase its bitterness.

## Challenges

The biggest growing challenge you'll have with radicchio is regulating moisture and temperature. Think high moisture and low temperature to get the sweetest results. If hot weather makes your radicchio bolt and grow a flower stalk instead of a head, clip it near the base to promote head growth.

**Pests:** As with cabbage and other lettuce-type plants, radicchio is prone to aphids, ants, and thrips. It's easy to brush off aphids and thrips, but for large outbreaks, use an insecticidal soap. To get rid of ants, apply peppermint oil as a barrier around your beds.

**Diseases:** Radicchio can develop various types of molds if not well-drained, so make sure the soil isn't too wet. Mold is hard to treat but removing infected leaves can help.

## Harvest it

Radicchio can be harvested when the heads are about the size of an orange or a grapefruit, depending on your preference. Even radicchio with a head the size of a tangerine is harvestable. A good rule of thumb is to begin harvesting when the heads are firm to the touch. And if you're growing a fall crop, harvest your plants after a few light frosts. The coolness helps improve the flavor. Regardless, don't wait too long. The older radicchio gets, the more bitter it becomes.

To harvest, clip the entire plant above the soil line or pick individual leaves as needed. The outer leaves are the most tender. To increase sweetness, blanch the heart. This involves putting a bag or box over the radicchio head a week before harvest until the leaves and stalks turn white. With a long-leafed variety, you can achieve the same effect by tying the leaves together in a tight pod on top of the plant.

**Store:** Harvested radicchio can be stored in the vegetable crisper for three or four weeks. To maximize freshness, keep it in a perforated plastic bag.

**Preserve:** I freeze radicchio to use in vegetable stocks and soups. Once thawed, its texture is too mushy for salads.

## Radicchio Salad with Oregano and Orange Vinaigrette

Sometimes the best salads are the simplest. The unique flavor of radicchio shines through here, with help from an orange and oregano dressing. Serves 6-8.

### Ingredients:

3 T red wine vinegar or apple cider vinegar

½ cup fresh squeezed orange juice

3 T olive oil

½ + ⅛ tsp salt

½ tsp black pepper

¾ tsp dried oregano

1 head radicchio, cut in half and chopped in 1-inch pieces

1 orange, sliced into 2-inch pieces

½ cup pistachios, shelled

### Preparation:

1.  Whisk together vinegar and orange juice.

2.  Whisk in olive oil, salt, pepper, and oregano, making sure to emulsify thoroughly.

3.  Place chopped radicchio, orange slices, and pistachios in a bowl, and toss with the vinaigrette.

# RHUBARB

**Rhubarb is a hardy vegetable that** prefers cool temperatures. Once established, it's pretty hard to get rid of. You can only eat the stalk because rhubarb leaves are poisonous.

**Varieties:** The variety of rhubarb you decide to plant will depend on how you want to use it. Some varieties, like Canada Red, are best for pies, while Sunrise, a pink stalk type, is better for canning and freezing. Common red-stalked rhubarb varieties include Valentine, Canada Red, Holstein Bloodred, Colorado Red, and Victoria, one of the sweeter varieties. German Wine is pink speckled and green, and Sutton Rhubarb is red and green streaked.

**Companion plants:** Onions and garlic pair nicely with rhubarb because they repel the aphids and other pests that feed on this plant. Avoid planting it with root crops like potatoes, turnips, and carrots because its extensive root structure will inhibit the other plants' ability to grow. Oxalic acid, the same ingredient that makes the leaves so toxic, works nicely as a pest deterrent. I've used water from boiled rhubarb leaves as a spray to prevent club rot root disease in broccoli, cabbage, and kale.

# Where it thrives

**Regional compatibility:** In order to be jolted into growth every spring rhubarb needs to first be exposed to cold weather. So rhubarb does best in cool regions like New England. In warm climates where winter temperatures rarely fall below 40 degrees, this vegetable is often grown as an annual.

**Optimal sun and shade:** Full sun is best for rhubarb growth in moderate to cool regions. Light partial shade and lots of water is better for growth and flavor in a warm climate.

**Soil type:** Rhubarb likes fertile soil that's heavy in organic matter. It also does best in a well-drained site.

**Resilience:** This vegetable benefits from occasional cold snaps and can withstand brief periods of drought. What rhubarb doesn't like is a lot of rain, which can result in stunted growth and thin, weak stalks. Mixing into the soil some compost or greensand (a mineral mixture rich in iron and potassium) or planting it in an elevated location that drains well can help keep the roots dry.

# Planting

**Best time of year to plant:** Plant rhubarb in the spring or fall. Spring is best if you live in a region with cold winters, while fall is better if you live in a warmer area. Plant rhubarb crowns when they're still dormant and the leaves have yet to emerge.

**From seeds:** Growing rhubarb from seed means it'll take longer to get a harvest. If you choose to go with seeds, plant them indoors in pots 8 to 10 weeks before the beginning of spring in cold regions, or before the chill of fall returns in warm areas. Push two or three seeds one-quarter inch deep into your pots. Remove all but the strongest plants before moving the seedlings outside. Since rhubarb likes cool weather, transplants can be set outside as early as two weeks before the last frost, as long as they're at least four inches tall.

**From cuttings:** Rhubarb is typically grown from crowns, which look like root stubs. Start by digging a hole about one foot by one foot. Before planting your crowns, work in one part compost to two parts soil. Make sure the roots are buried two to four inches beneath the soil line and at least four feet apart. Your rhubarb will eventually take up a lot of space.

## Growing

Once rhubarb is established, it grows quickly and requires little tending. In fact, rhubarb is so resilient, it's hard to get rid of. I once had a monster plant that cast such a large shadow it stunted neighboring plants. I used a harvest knife to cut it down to the soil. In exactly one month, all of it was back. So I chopped it down again. And again. In the end I gave up and decided the best way to keep my rhubarb contained was to make more pies.

**Weeding:** The most important time to weed the area around rhubarb is when you're planting the seeds.

**Watering:** Young rhubarb needs a lot of moisture to survive, particularly in the summertime. Mature rhubarb needs much less water, but the large leaves can bake in the sun. In most regions of the country you can get away with one good soak a week. Aim to wet the soil at least four inches deep.

**Fertilizing after planting:** Rhubarb's giant leaves need a lot of nitrogen to sustain vigorous growth. Each spring, add a big heap of compost as well as a high-nitrogen fertilizer like composted manure or blood meal. Compost works well because it adds nitrogen and other nutrients to the soil for the next growing season.

## Challenges

This is a low-maintenance plant, but every five or six years you'll need to divide it or it will stop thriving. Lift each crown, typically with a garden fork. Split it into three or four pieces and replant. If you don't want more rhubarb in your garden, share the crowns with your neighbors.

**Pests:** Rhubarb leaves can be damaged by aphids, thrips, or beetles, but this isn't a big deal because it won't affect the rhubarb flavor. If you keep your rhubarb weed-free, pests won't be an issue.

**Diseases:** Rhubarb is susceptible to crown rot. To prevent this, plant it in a well-drained place. Once plants are infected, it's impossible to get rid of the disease. You'll have to dig up your compromised crowns and get rid of them. Don't replant rhubarb in the same place where you found crown rot.

## Harvest it

Hold off on harvesting your rhubarb for the first year so it has a chance to mature and develop its root system. Rhubarb stalks can be harvested when they're between 12 and 18 inches long. Mature rhubarb has an optimal harvest period that lasts about two months. To harvest, twist and pull the stalk at its base or simply cut it. If you remove all the leaves, rhubarb will struggle to regrow the next season, so leave two to three stalks on each plant.

**Store:** Make sure you cut off and dispose of the poisonous leafy tops! Rhubarb stalks can be kept up to one week in the refrigerator if stored properly. Wrap the stalks in plastic but don't wash them until just before using.

**Preserve:** Rhubarb is easy to turn into jam or to freeze. Cut the stalks into one-inch pieces and spread them on a baking sheet. Freeze for 15 minutes before transferring the frozen stalks into a plastic bag.

# Rhubarb and Apple Pie

While you can bake this pie without pre-cooking the rhubarb, poaching the vegetable makes it easier to work with and adds to the tangy sweetness. Save this recipe for a rainy day. Serves 6-8.

## Ingredients:

*For poached rhubarb:*

3 cups water

1 ½ cups sugar

Juice of 1 tangerine or orange

1 T lemon juice

2 T brandy

1 tsp vanilla

¼ tsp whole cloves

1 cinnamon stick

1 lb rhubarb, cut into 1-inch pieces

3 medium-size apples, sliced

Your favorite pie dough, chilled

Egg wash

Sugar for topping

## Preparation:

1. In a medium-size saucepan, mix water, sugar, juices, brandy, vanilla, cloves, and cinnamon. Bring to a boil, then let simmer for 10 minutes.

2. Poach the rhubarb in 2 batches until fork tender, about 10 minutes.

3. Spoon rhubarb into a large bowl, and save the liquid.

4. Mix apple slices with the cooked rhubarb.

## To bake pie:

1. Grease a 9- or 10-inch pie plate. Roll out ⅔ of pie dough and place in pie plate. Poke the dough a few times with the tines of a fork. (Keep remaining pie dough in fridge until ready to use.)

2. Add rhubarb/apple filling.

3. Roll out remaining pie dough and place on top of filling. Seal and crimp pie edges, and make a few 1-inch cuts in the dough (to release steam while baking).

4. Brush top of pie with egg wash and sprinkle with sugar.

5. Bake in oven for 40 minutes, or until crust is a deep golden brown.

# SPINACH

**Perennial spinach is not related to** common spinach, but it has a similar taste and can be cooked in the same way. The triangular and somewhat fuzzy leaves are valued for their high concentration of vitamin C. Unlike common spinach, this tender perennial does well in the summer heat, so it's a nice choice for warm-weather gardeners.

**Varieties:** Types of perennial spinach include New Zealand Spinach, also known as Tetragonia, which sprawls across the ground. You can also find it in seed catalogs as Maori Spinach.

**Companion plants:** This leafy green can grow alongside just about any plant in the garden, but don't pair it with tall, sun-blocking plants, like beans and corn, since it doesn't do as well in shade.

## Where it thrives

**Regional compatibility:** Perennial spinach is perennial only in mild, frost-free winter locations. In other climates, it's grown as a summer annual.

**Optimal sun and shade:** Full sun, at least five to six hours a day, is best for this vegetable. The leaves are bigger when grown in partial shade, but the plant will also grow more slowly.

**Soil type:** Perennial spinach prefers soil that is sandy, well-drained, and rich in compost. But it's not that picky and can grow in dense soil, too.

**Resilience:** A heat-loving green that thrives even when temperatures soar over 90 degrees, perennial spinach can turn to mush in the lightest frost. The plant is very drought-tolerant and, while it won't grow to its full potential in dry conditions, it will still produce scrumptious greens. It can also tolerate salty soil and short periods of flooding.

## Planting

**Best time of year to plant:** Plant it in spring after the last frost. If you live in a cooler region, you may need to start your spinach indoors and move it outside when the weather warms up.

**From seeds:** In cooler regions with short growing seasons, it's best to start this plant inside six to eight weeks before the last spring frost. Waiting for spinach seeds to germinate can take up to three weeks. To speed things along, soak the seeds overnight or scarify them by rubbing them with sandpaper. Roughing up the outer coating makes it easier for water to enter the seed and prompt growth. Plant seeds a half-inch deep. Wait to transplant your seedlings outside until daytime temperatures are above 65 degrees.

In warm climates with a long growing season, go ahead and plant seeds directly in the garden. Keep the soil moist and weed-free while waiting for the seeds to take hold. Plants won't really take off until summer kicks in and nighttime temperatures climb above 60 degrees.

**From cuttings:** Perennial spinach is best grown from seed.

# Growing

Perennial spinach typically grows rapidly in midsummer when it's hottest. Since this weak-stemmed plant doesn't have the structural support to stand up, it creeps along the ground, growing several feet wide but only one foot tall. There's no need to prune it.

**Weeding:** This perennial has few problems with weeds once it's fully grown. Mulch the soil with about two inches of straw or hay to fight off weeds and conserve moisture.

**Watering:** Once perennial spinach is established, it doesn't need much water. But the warmer the region, the more water it needs. A good general rule is to soak the soil until the top two inches are wet. Thirsty plants often flower, or bolt, giving the succulent leaves a slightly bitter taste.

**Fertilizing after planting:** This fast-growing plant depends on a healthy supply of nitrogen. Composted manure from grass-grazing animals, like cows and sheep, is a great organic source of nitrogen, as are chicken droppings. Make sure the manure is composted because fresh manure contains a lot of weed seeds. If manure is too messy, consider using blood meal, but only on mature plants because it can easily burn tender seedlings.

# Challenges

This plant needs hot and humid weather to really take off. If your plant seems sluggish and slow to grow, it probably isn't hot enough where you live. If you need to give your plants more warmth, try planting them close to a house, fence, or stone wall that can absorb and share heat.

**Pests:** Perennial spinach is essentially pest-resistant. Even slugs and snails seem to leave it alone.

**Diseases:** Fungal mildews like downy or powdery mildew can infect perennial spinach. The mildews appear as round dots that cover the leaves and give your spinach a festive polka dot appearance. Infected leaves can still be eaten. Spray the leaves with neem or sulfur to slow the spread of fungus.

## Harvest it

Perennial spinach can be harvested as soon as the plant is six inches high. Simply cut off the leaves with sharp scissors. The smaller the leaf, the more tender it will be.

**Store:** Store harvested leaves by wrapping them in a damp paper towel in a plastic bag, and refrigerating. Otherwise the succulent leaves will dry out quickly.

**Preserve:** Leaves can be frozen (fresh or blanched) and kept in a ziplock bag for up to a year.

# Pasta with Perennial Spinach

Who doesn't love a one bowl meal? Pick your favorite pasta, toss in some iron-rich spinach, a few salty olives, and grated pecorino, and you're good to go. Serves 2.

## Ingredients

½ lb short pasta

Pinch of chili pepper flakes

1 clove garlic, finely minced

Olive oil

12-15 Kalamata or other olives, pitted and roughly chopped

4 generous handfuls spinach

Freshly grated nutmeg

Salt

Pepper

Parmesan or pecorino, freshly grated

## Preparation:

1. Cook pasta al dente.

2. In a skillet, saute chili pepper and garlic in olive oil for 1 minute. Add olives.

3. Add the spinach to the skillet, sprinkle with nutmeg, and cook over medium heat; stir, and let it soften just a little. Remove from heat.

4. Drain pasta, keeping a small amount of the starchy cooking water (makes it silkier) and add to skillet. Toss to combine. Cook over low heat, and sprinkle with pepper.

5. Divide between 2 warmed pasta bowls, top with grated cheese, and serve immediately.

# SUNCHOKE

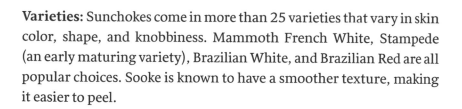

**Sunchoke is also known as Jerusalem** artichoke. A type of perennial sunflower, sunchoke is grown for its edible knobby root, which resembles a potato. It has a delicate nutty, crunchy taste and can be eaten raw or cooked. The plant is so hardy, it can be grown almost anywhere. Another perk for gardeners: watching the bright yellow flowers rotate as they track the sun across the sky.

**Varieties:** Sunchokes come in more than 25 varieties that vary in skin color, shape, and knobbiness. Mammoth French White, Stampede (an early maturing variety), Brazilian White, and Brazilian Red are all popular choices. Sooke is known to have a smoother texture, making it easier to peel.

**Companion plants:** Sunchokes attract aphids but aren't harmed by them because the bugs go after the leaves, not the edible roots. This makes these plants a great asset to a garden because they lure bugs away from more delicate plants. Sunchokes also grow well with cucumbers and beans, which use the sturdy flower stalks as a natural trellis. Another benefit of sunchokes: they provide shade for heat-sensitive plants, like lettuce and spinach. Avoid planting sunchokes with other root crops because they'll compete for space underground.

## Where it thrives

**Regional compatibility:** Sunchokes are native to eastern North America and can be grown just about anywhere. They do equally well in the Texas heat and on the frozen plains of New Brunswick, but the plant is most productive in northern, cooler regions.

**Optimal sun and shade:** Sunchokes need about six hours of full sun a day to produce big roots. You can grow them in partial shade, but the tubers will be much smaller.

**Soil type:** As with most tubers, sunchokes prefer loose, sandy soil that allows the roots to expand easily. They also do just fine in nutrient-poor, rocky soils. If your soil is hard packed or contains lots of clay, you'll grow tiny sunchokes that are difficult to harvest. You can loosen up dense soil by adding compost and organic matter.

**Resilience:** Hardy and versatile plants, sunchokes are somewhat drought-resistant. But they need to be watered at least once a week if you want a big crop of these tasty tubers. Although they can withstand lots of rain, wind, and heat, prolonged flooding will lead to rot.

## Planting

**Best time of year to plant:** Plant sunchokes as soon as the soil has warmed up in the spring.

**From seeds:** It is possible to grow sunchokes from seed, but the plants tend not to produce the big, vigorous tubers you want. Most gardeners work with seed tubers instead.

**From cuttings:** Order seed tubers, or slips, in the early spring and store them in a cool place until you're ready to plant. If you want more than one sunchoke from each tuber, use a clean, sharp knife to cut the tuber so each piece has at least two eyes. An eye is the dimple on the skin where a shoot forms to become the leafy part of the plant. Avoid cutting each tuber into more than two pieces because too many cuts can leave the tubers susceptible to fungal disease. Before planting, let the cut tubers heal, or scab over, for a few days. You can also just plant the tubers whole. Regardless, plant them 6 inches deep and 12 inches apart. Once established, they're hard to remove so think carefully about where you want them.

## Growing

Sunchokes have a tall, sunflower-like bloom that serves as a beautiful garden windbreak and natural trellis. These easy-to-grow plants need no pruning. In colder regions, cover them in the fall with a layer of protective straw mulch. When spring arrives, top the leftover mulch with fresh compost to prep the plants for the growing season.

**Weeding:** Sunchokes grow tall enough that they often shade out weeds. But keep an eye out for any early spring weeds that could take hold before your plants take off.

**Watering:** This no-fuss plant usually gets enough water from rain. If you live in a particularly dry area, plan on watering your plant but no more than an inch a week. Let the soil dry out between waterings. Overwatering sunchokes can bring on rot.

**Fertilizing after planting:** Sunchokes flourish with a good supply of potassium, which you can provide with a well-balanced 10-10-10 fertilizer, wood ash, or greensand. Greensand is a potassium-rich mineral soil found on the ocean floor. Avoid using high-nitrogen fertilizers or the tops will grow thick and lush at the expense of root development.

# Challenges

The sunchoke can become invasive. Since it is nearly impossible to harvest every single tuber, there will always be volunteer plants the following spring. The best non-chemical way to get rid of sunchokes is to destroy all the volunteer plants in late summer before they set tubers. You can also avoid the whole problem by simply growing your tubers in a large container.

**Pests:** Sunchokes are burly tubers that resist most pests in the summer. Wireworms, which live in the soil, can tunnel into the root and damage the tubers. Wireworms are only a problem if you plant in once-grassy areas.

The sunflower maggot can also bore inside the stem, destroying the plant's ability to bring in water and nutrients and eventually killing it. This pest is hard to eradicate because most of the time you don't know it's there until the plant falls over and dies. Plus, they hide in the soil through the winter. If you have a problem with either of these pests, you might have to pull out as many healthy tubers as you can save and try planting them somewhere else.

**Diseases:** Prevent white mold rot by planting your sunchokes in well-drained areas. Soggy tubers can become moldy tubers. Downy mildew can also be a problem in areas with high humidity, but it only affects the leaves; the tubers will stay safe underground.

# Harvest it

Sunchoke tubers are ready to be picked in the fall. If you wait until after the first frost, they'll taste a little sweeter. To prep your tubers, step on the stems once flowers appear and bend them to divert energy from the leaves to the tubers. When the leaves die, the tubers are ready to harvest.

**Store:** Sunchokes can keep in the refrigerator for a few weeks when wrapped in paper towels and sealed in a plastic bag.

**Preserve:** This tuber's shelf life is almost as long as a potato's. Sunchokes will last three to five months in a cool, dry, and dark location, like a basement or the back of your kitchen pantry.

## Roasted Sunchokes

Roasted sunchokes are a nice replacement for potatoes in recipes because they're snappy and sweet, with a crunchy exterior and soft interior. The curry powder in this dish complements the natural sweetness of the sunchokes. Serves 6 as a side dish.

### Ingredients:

3 cups sunchokes, sliced into 1-inch pieces

1 T olive oil

1 ½ tsp curry powder

½ tsp sea salt

¼ tsp black pepper

### Preparation:

1.  Preheat oven to 375 degrees.

2.  Toss sunchokes in olive oil and spices.

3.  Spread on a baking sheet and roast for 25 minutes.

# SWEET POTATO

**Sweet potatoes thrive in climates from one** extreme to the other. While not related to yams, they're often mislabeled as such in grocery stores. These colorful tubers are packed with beta carotene and a nutritious alternative to white potatoes.

**Varieties:** Sweet potato comes in orange-, purple-, and white-fleshed varieties. Nancy Hall is an orange variety that grows best in warm regions. Georgia Jet does well in cool regions. And Beauregard grows just about anywhere. For purple sweet potatoes, try Bonita, O'Henry, and Sumor. For white, you'll want Violetta or All Purple.

**Companion plants:** Good companion plants for sweet potatoes include aromatic herbs like dill and thyme, which help keep away pests. Avoid planting sweet potatoes with squash because both need a lot of room to spread out.

# Where it thrives

**Regional compatibility:** Although sweet potatoes can be successfully grown in cooler, northern regions of the United States, they do best where the summers are long and hot.

**Optimal sun and shade:** These tropical plants prefer about eight hours of full sun a day.

**Soil type:** Sweet potatoes like a mildly acidic soil in a well-drained, warm site. Potatoes grown in alkaline or basic soils are more susceptible to disease, and good drainage helps prevent the tubers from rot. They can grow in compact clay soils but will be rough and irregularly shaped rather than uniform in size.

**Resilience:** These sweet tubers prefer hot, humid weather to a cool, frosty climate and are not particularly drought-tolerant. They also won't grow well in salty soil.

# Planting

**Best time of year to plant:** Plant your sweet potatoes in the spring after the weather heats up. Soil that's about 60 to 85 degrees warm is important for their growth.

**From seeds:** Sweet potatoes are not grown from seeds.

**From cuttings:** The sweet potato equivalent of cuttings are shoots that sprout from a mature potato. You can either buy shoots or sprout them from store-bought tubers. To grow sweet potatoes from other sweet potatoes, clean your tubers and cut them in half. Use toothpicks to suspend the potato piece, cut face down, over a bowl of water, lightly touching the surface. Keep the bowl in a warm place and you'll soon see shoots growing.

Once the shoots are five inches long, gently snap them off. Place each shoot in another shallow bowl of water so the stem is submerged and the leaf end hangs out of the bowl. Within a few days, you'll see root hairs growing from the stem. These are slips. Keep them healthy by changing the water daily and discarding the ones that aren't producing roots or are wilting. The slips are ready to plant when the roots are about an inch long. Choose a warm, sunny site and plant them 12 to 18 inches apart.

There's an even simpler way to start sweet potatoes: buy some from the grocery story, dig a trench, toss them in, and cover them up with soil. The deeper you plant your tubers, the more sweet potatoes you'll harvest.

## Growing

In warm areas, sweet potatoes grow quickly, within two weeks of planting. Where it's cool, you can warm up the soil by applying a heavy layer of mulch after planting.

**Weeding:** Avoid planting sweet potatoes in grassy, or formerly grassy, areas. Grass-loving pests may come back to feast on them.

**Watering:** Water your sweet potatoes thoroughly and frequently, particularly in the first month of growth. After the vines become long enough to trail, give them an inch of water a week. Avoid overwatering by letting the soil dry out fully or the tubers may rot.

**Fertilizing after planting:** Sweet potatoes love soil rich in organic matter. Each spring, dress the top of the soil with a thin layer of compost. Mix in some kelp meal as well to add the potassium sweet potatoes need to flourish.

## Challenges

Sweet potatoes may prefer hot and humid regions, but I've been growing sweet potatoes in New England for years. It's only in far northern, less sunny areas, like northern Maine, Alaska, and coastal Washington, where these tubers have trouble growing.

**Pests:** The sweet flesh of these potatoes attracts pests, like the larval form of beetles that feed on the tubers, creating holes and tunnels that can produce rot. Moles, voles, and mice also love to gnaw on tubers. Various caterpillars, like armyworms and hornworms, concentrate on the sweet potato foliage. Control them by spraying the leaves with Bt, a natural soil bacteria, or with an insecticidal soap.

**Diseases:** Fungal and bacterial rot can damage the roots. Fusarium wilt stunts the vines and creates hard, dark spots on the potatoes. Prevention is the best defense, so plant your tubers in well-drained soil. Make sure never to replant infected tubers or use them to produce slips because disease can be passed along to the next generation.

## Harvest it

Dig up sweet potato roots in the summer and fall while the weather is still warm. Once the leaves start to wither and turn yellow, your tubers are ready to be harvested. Gently loosen the soil with a pitchfork so you disturb it as little as possible while pulling up the tubers.

**Store:** Store sweet potatoes at room temperature, preferably in a dark place.

**Preserve:** Curing sweet potatoes makes them sweeter because of a chemical process that turns some of the potato starch into sugar. To cure them, keep your potatoes in a warm, humid place for two weeks.

Then wrap each sweet potato in newspaper and store it in a cool place (55–60 degrees). Cured sweet potatoes can be stored for up to 10 months.

## Thick-Cut Sweet Potato Fries

Serve these healthy baked fries with a chipotle aioli or homemade ketchup. You could even try a sweet potato poutine for a spin on a Canadian favorite. Serves 6-8 as a side dish.

### Ingredients:

2-4 large sweet potatoes

Olive oil

Salt

Pepper

Cumin

### Preparation:

1.  Preheat oven to 375 degrees. Slice potatoes in half if they're long, then cut into 1-inch wedges. Keep the skin to add texture and nutrients.

2.  Drizzle with olive oil and toss with salt and pepper. Add a few pinches of cumin.

3.  Roast in oven for 20 minutes, or until easily pierced with a fork.

# TOMATO

**Countless tomato varieties exist, from** tangy and tart to sweet, from big and red to cherry-sized. Heat-loving tomatoes need a long growing season, so plan accordingly. While typically grown as annuals, tomatoes are tender perennials in frost-free climates. If you live in a cold region, bring your tomatoes inside before the first frost to enjoy the taste of summer all year long.

**Varieties:** Tomatoes come in a wide assortment of shapes, colors, and sizes. To wade through the endless list of varieties, consider how much space you have and when you want to harvest.

Tomatoes considered indeterminate are climbing varieties that need to be staked or trellised. Under ideal conditions, some of these plants can grow 12 feet high so give them plenty of space. The fruit ripens all summer long, giving you a steady supply of delicious tomatoes. Determinant plants are bush varieties that are more compact and require less staking. Their fruits ripen all at once. These are a good choice if you're a new gardener or planning to grow your plants in containers.

Once you choose between vining or bush, you can decide whether you want to grow cherry tomatoes (perfect for salads and fresh summer snacks), paste tomatoes (great for homemade pasta sauce and roasting), or beefsteak tomatoes (delicious sliced onto veggie burgers and sandwiches).

**Companion plants:** Tomatoes grow best with chives, onion, and parsley because the strong-smelling herbs repel bugs. They also do well with marigolds and nasturtiums, which act as host plants for aphids, a common tomato pest. Raising them along with basil can actually improve their growth and flavor.

## Where it thrives

**Regional compatibility:** Tomatoes like long, hot summers with plenty of sun, but different varieties have adapted to grow just about anywhere. For cooler climates, consider growing early-maturing varieties, like Amish Gold.

**Optimal sun and shade:** Tomatoes need about eight hours a day of direct sunlight to be fruitful.

**Soil type:** These tender perennials prefer sandy loam soils with good drainage but can be grown in almost any type of soil, except heavy clay.

**Resilience:** Tomatoes adapt readily to drought conditions once they've matured. In fact, tomatoes grown without much water tend to be higher in nutritional value than those grown with lots of water. Some varieties are more drought-tolerant than others. Cherry tomatoes, for example, require less water than the huge beefsteak varieties. What affects tomatoes more than water is how hot or cold it is. Frost will destroy your plants.

# Planting

**Best time of year to plant:** Tomatoes need warm weather to grow, so start seedlings inside in the spring. To plant them outside, you'd have to wait until May or June, which doesn't give the fruit enough time to ripen.

**From seeds:** Five or six weeks before the last frost, sow seeds about a quarter-inch deep in two-inch pots. To help the seeds germinate more quickly, arrange your pots on a heating mat set at 80 degrees. Be careful not to let your pots dry out and remove them from the heat mat once the seeds have germinated to prevent leggy stems.

Tomatoes can handle a few cool nights, but it's safer to move them outside after nighttime temperatures have warmed to at least 55 degrees. In the week before the move, introduce your seedlings to the outdoors gradually so they get used to it. Leave your plants outside during the day and bring them back inside at night.

Once it's time to put your seedlings in the ground, space climbing varieties one to two feet apart and bushy varieties two to three feet apart. If you want to set out your plants early while the nights are still cool, protect them with a row cover. Make sure to remove the cover every morning or you might fry your plants.

To help your plants develop an extensive root system, plant them deep in the soil about one inch from the first true leaves. Tomatoes can grow roots from the tiny hairs that cover the stem, and burying the stem triggers more root growth, which makes the plants more resilient. You can also enhance root development by clipping the flowers until your plants are a foot tall. By delaying fruit production, you'll encourage your plants to devote their energy to growing more roots.

**From cuttings:** Tomatoes are best grown from seed.

# Growing

All tomatoes benefit from being staked or trellised because keeping them off the ground limits the risk of pest damage and disease. Prune your climbing plants to one or two central stalks and tie them to a sturdy bamboo stake. The small shoots that grow out of the joint where the leaf meets the stem are called suckers. Remove them so more energy flows into the fruit-bearing central stem. If you don't want sticky yellow hands, wear gloves. Bushy varieties are shorter but still benefit from being staked or supported by a tomato cage. This keeps the branches off the ground and the fruit away from the soil.

**Weeding:** Keep your plants weed-free until they mature. Once established, healthy tomato plants shouldn't need much weeding.

**Watering:** The secret to growing flavorful tomatoes is to go easy on the watering. Wet them thoroughly once a week as the plants mature. Unless you live in a very hot and dry region, stop watering once the tomatoes start to develop, which is usually by the beginning of August. They'll continue to ripen into the fall even after the vines begin to wilt. In the sorts of places where the soil cracks from being so dry, you'll have to water tomatoes even as the fruits ripen. But avoid watering on harvest days so you can pick the tomatoes at their most flavorful.

**Fertilizing after planting:** Tomatoes are heavy feeders and require more nutrients than your average plant. Before planting, mix into your soil compost and a fertilizer high in nitrogen, like blood meal. To encourage an abundant crop, add a phosphorus fertilizer, like bone meal, after the first tomatoes have appeared. Tomatoes can suffer from blossom end rot when there's either not enough calcium in the soil or the moisture varies a lot. If you notice black and brown leathery patches at the blossom end of fruits, add calcium in the form of lime. Infected fruit is still delicious—just cut out the brown spots.

# Challenges

Tomatoes are happiest when temperatures range between 70 and 95 degrees during the day and 55 and 70 degrees at night. If temperatures are too hot or too cold, the plants may drop their blossoms and no fruit will form.

**Pests:** Tomato hornworms are green caterpillars that can quickly eat most of the leaves off a tomato plant. The worms can be picked off but their green color makes them hard to spot. Use an insecticidal soap or Bt to get rid of them.

The wireworm can be deadly to newly transplanted tomato plants. Wireworms are the larval stage of click beetles. They tend to be a problem if your garden bed used to be part of a lawn or is close to a lawn. Wireworms feast on the stems of plants. Damaged plants will wither and die before you even realize what's happened. To get rid of these pests, bury a potato attached to a stick four or five inches deep in your soil. After three weeks, dig up your potato trap and remove all the worms you've captured. (Wireworms love potatoes.) You're ready to plant tomatoes!

**Diseases:** Verticillium and fusarium wilts are soil-borne diseases that can kill plants fast. Once the soil has become infected with these diseases, it's nearly impossible to prevent damage to tomato plants. If you spot signs of wilt, make sure not to plant tomatoes in that area for at least five years.

Blight is a fungal disease that can damage young and mature plants early or late in the season. There's little you can do about blight once plants have it, but you can keep the disease from invading the stems by removing infected leaves. Don't compost the infected leaves or the fungal infection will spread.

# Harvest it

Pick your fruit as soon as it's ripe. The more you pick, the more tomatoes you'll have. Use scissors or your fingers to break the fruit from the plant at the knuckle, also called a peduncle. This is its weak joint. Once fall temperatures threaten the vitality of your tomato plant, pick whatever green fruit remains and bring it inside to ripen.

**Store:** Store your tomatoes out of direct sunlight. Do not refrigerate or they'll become mealy and flavorless.

**Preserve:** Once thawed, frozen tomatoes become mushy, but they're still good for sauces and cooked foods.

# Roasted Tomato Soup

Roasting tomatoes bring out their flavor. Serve this simple soup with salad and a toasted baguette. Serves 4.

## Ingredients:

2 ½ pounds fresh tomatoes, stemmed and quartered

1 medium white onion, cut into thick slices

4 cloves garlic, sliced in half

½ cup good quality extra virgin olive oil

Salt

Pepper

4 cups vegetable stock

2 bay leaves

½ cup fresh chopped basil leaves or 1 T dried basil

## Preparation:

1. Preheat oven to 375 degrees. Spread tomatoes and onions on a baking sheet. Add garlic and sprinkle with salt and pepper. Drizzle ¼ cup of the olive oil over the vegetables and roast for 20 minutes.

2. Transfer to a large stock pot. Add remaining ¼ cup olive oil, vegetable stock, and bay leaves. Bring to a boil, then reduce heat to low. Let simmer for 15-20 minutes.

3. Remove bay leaves and add basil.

4. With an immersion blender or working in batches with a regular blender, puree until smooth. Serve hot.

# WALKING ONION

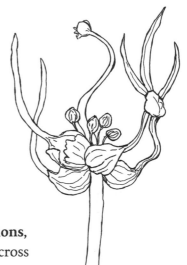

**Walking onions, also known as top onions,** are a delicious perennial. They "walk" across the garden thanks to tiny bulbs called topsets. These form at the tip of the leaves, making the plant bend over and fall. The fallen topsets then root and grow into mature plants the following season. The entire plant can be eaten, from the shallot-like roots to the topsets and hollow leaves.

**Varieties:** The most common variety is the Egyptian Walking Onion, but you can also find Merceron Red Catawissa and Fleener's Top-Setting Onion in some seed catalogs.

**Companion plants:** Onions smell so strong they help protect plants from insects and other pests, like rabbits. Sprinkle walking onions all around your garden.

## Where it thrives

**Regional compatibility:** Walking onions are extremely hardy and can withstand very cold winters. I've harvested bulbs in the dead of winter and while they've lost their snap, the thawed bulbs taste just fine. The plant does okay in warm climates but doesn't fare well in hot and humid summers. Instead of tasty topset bulbs, you might get flowers instead.

**Optimal sun and shade:** Walking onions thrive with six hours of full sun a day. In hotter regions, afternoon shade helps prevent heat stress.

**Soil type:** These plants do well in light loam or sandy soils that are acidic. Good drainage will prevent the bulbs from rotting.

**Resilience:** Walking onions are very drought-tolerant and, once established, need no help flourishing. The bulb at the base of the plant will be smaller and more pungent in dry conditions but delicious nonetheless.

## Planting

**Best time of year to plant:** Plant walking onions anytime after the ground has thawed and before the first fall frost.

**From seeds:** Walking onions don't produce seeds.

**From cuttings:** Walking onions are best grown from topsets, its version of cuttings. No need to start your new plants indoors. This plant is tough. Plant the bulbs in the ground about two inches deep and they'll grow. It's as simple as that. The only thing that prevents this little plant from growing is prolonged flooding or mucky soil.

## Growing

Walking onions are also called "forever onions" because, once established, they keep growing with little to no help. To keep your onions in check, keep the topsets from taking root once they fall over. Add mulch in the fall to protect the shallow bulbs from hard winter freezes.

**Weeding:** Weeds compete with regular onions for water and nutrients, but they're no threat to this hardy plant.

**Watering:** Walking onions don't need much watering, though you can help them take root and grow more quickly if you give them about an inch of water a week. Let your soil dry out between waterings because otherwise the bulb may rot.

**Fertilizing:** Walking onions will grow even in lifeless dirt. But if you want to keep these plants really happy, go ahead and add a layer of compost each spring.

## Challenges

The only problem you'll have with walking onions is trying to keep them from spreading all over your garden. Thankfully, they're easy to pull out and even easier to introduce into your dinner recipes.

**Pests:** The strong odor of onion plants is a deterrent to most pests. Occasionally, onion thrips and maggots can be a problem, but they're easily treated with neem oil. Branching topsets make a great place for spiders to hang out. I love the misty mornings when I can see the intricate webs outlined in glistening dew.

**Diseases:** Various rots, including fusarium basal rot, can plague the walking onion. If your onions become infected with rot, make sure to prevent them from "walking," or rerooting, so they don't spread the disease.

# Harvest it

You can harvest every part of this amazing plant. Go ahead and pick the hollow green leaves as soon as they sprout in the spring. Chop them up and eat them like chives or green onions. The topsets are ready to go as soon as the stalk bends over in mid-summer. Harvest the shallot roots in late summer. I recommend eating them peeled and fried, but you can prepare them just as you would any other onion or shallot.

**Store:** It's best to eat the greens immediately because they don't keep for very long. But the shallot-like onion that forms at the base can be kept at room temperature for up to three weeks.

**Preserve:** You can freeze the greens in a plastic bag for up to five months. My favorite way to preserve topsets is to pickle them. Spicy!

# Fried Walking Onions

Walking onions crisp up nicely. Serve them as appetizers or for a game day party. They're fine as is, or served with your favorite ranch or green goddess dressing as a dip. Serves 4.

## Ingredients:

12-15 walking onions (bulbs)

1 cup buttermilk or nondairy milk

1 cup flour

¼ cup cornmeal

1 tsp garlic powder

1 teaspoon onion powder

½ tsp salt

½ tsp black pepper

## Preparation:

1. Slice ends from onions and remove outer layer. On one side of each onion, make two cuts, lengthwise and crosswise, while keeping the bottom intact. Peel back slightly.

2. Pour milk into a small bowl.

3. In another bowl, whisk together flour, cornmeal, and spices.

4. In a large wok or dutch oven, heat 3 inches of vegetable oil to 350 degrees.

5. Dunk each onion in the milk, then dredge in the flour mixture until evenly coated.

6. Fry in hot oil for 3 minutes, or until crispy.

7. Drain on paper towels or a cooling rack set over a baking pan.

# WATERCRESS

**Watercress is a bona fide power food packed with vitamins** A, C, and K. It's fairly adaptable and easy to grow—unless you live in a desert. This water-loving member of the cabbage and mustard family makes a flavorful addition to a variety of dishes and salads.

**Varieties:** Watercress is divided into four major categories, depending on how bitter and peppery the greens taste. Garden Cress has a sweet yet spicy bite similar to horseradish. Korean Watercress has a great crunch when eaten raw and is the least bitter of the cress varieties. Nasturtium Watercress has lily pad-shaped leaves, hollow stems, and bright green foliage, while Upland Cress has a mild flavor with a delicate peppery aftertaste.

**Companion plants:** It's hard to find a good companion for watercress because it thrives in wet soils, which most plants don't appreciate. If you can find a happy medium between waterlogged and moist soil, watercress will pair well with chives, peppermint, spearmint, and wintergreen, all of which tolerate soggy soil conditions.

# Where it thrives

**Regional compatibility:** Watercress does best in moist, cool climates but it can grow well in warm climates if located near cool, flowing water.

**Optimal sun and shade:** This plant prefers full sun but will do fine in shade.

**Soil type:** Watercress thrives in moist soil that ranges from basic (7.5 pH) to acidic (5.5 pH). Typically found near or in creeks, the plant also grows well in somewhat sandy soil that is heavily mulched.

**Resilience:** This water-loving plant can survive flooding and needs lots of watering to survive drought.

# Planting

**Best time of year to plant:** Plant in the spring or early fall.

**From seeds:** To start seeds, sprinkle them on the surface of your container where they can get the light they need to germinate. Gently pat them into the soil. The seeds should sprout within two weeks. Seeds can also be sown directly into the garden once temperatures are above 48 degrees.

**From cuttings:** If you want your watercress to grow more quickly, buy some from the grocery store and soak the ends in water. Change the water daily and eventually roots will appear. Plant these cuttings in the soil about three inches apart.

# Growing

Watercress is essentially a weed that flourishes along streams. If it can grow unattended in the wild, surely you can grow it in your garden. To help it along, pinch off the top shoots to encourage bushy branching once the plant is six inches tall. If you choose to grow your watercress in a container, keep it well watered and in a cool, shady location.

**Weeding:** Clear the area around watercress so thirsty weeds don't suck up the water it needs to grow.

**Watering:** Either plant it in a very moist area or plan to water it most days.

**Fertilizing after planting:** Watercress loves compost-rich soil, which helps keep it moist. If you plant watercress in sandy soil, give it some compost in the spring and late summer.

# Challenges

The biggest growing challenge is making sure your cress gets enough water. If there's a particularly wet, low area of your garden—or even better, a nearby stream—plant your watercress there. If not, make sure it's well-watered throughout the growing season.

**Pests:** Watercress is susceptible to aphids. Hose them off gently—you don't want to damage the leaves with a high-pressure stream of water—and they shouldn't be a problem.

**Diseases:** If growing watercress near a stream or other body of water, make sure the water is clean. Otherwise, the plant can pick up bacteria and other pathogens, becoming dangerous for human consumption.

# Harvest it

Watercress can be harvested throughout the year, starting as soon as six to eight weeks after you sow seeds. Harvest the crispest, darkest, and most mature leaves first. They have a fresh, peppery, rich, and slightly bitter taste. If you want to add some nutritional heft to your diet, consider chopping and drying the leaves so you can sprinkle them on your food.

**Store:** Watercress is best stored in a glass or bowl of water with the stems submerged and the tops covered by plastic wrap. The leaves can also be refrigerated in a plastic bag, ideally in the vegetable crisper. Both these methods can keep watercress fresh for up to a week.

**Preserve:** Separate the leaves from stems and dry them out.

# Watercress Salad with Avocado, Cucumber, and Red Onion

A simple lemon-Dijon vinaigrette accentuates the delicate texture and peppery flavor of watercress. Makes 1 large salad that can serve 4-6.

## Ingredients:

1 ½ cups lightly chopped watercress (include stems)

2 cups shredded kale (or other crunchy lettuce)

1 small cucumber, sliced lengthwise and cut in ¼-inch pieces

¾ cup red onion, diced

½ medium-size avocado

*Lemon-Dijon dressing:*

2 T olive oil

2 T lemon juice

1 T honey

1 T water

1 T Dijon mustard

¼ tsp salt

⅛ tsp pepper

## Preparation:

1. In a large bowl, toss together watercress, kale, cucumber, red onion, and avocado.

2. In a medium-sized bowl, whisk together olive oil, lemon juice, and honey. Add water and mustard, then salt and pepper, whisking to thoroughly combine.

3. Lightly toss salad with dressing.

# FREQUENTLY ASKED QUESTIONS

## I don't have a yard. Can I still grow good food?

Don't let a lack of space or an urban setting stop you from participating in the carbon capture movement. An excellent way to get your hands dirty is to sign up for a community garden. Or offer to help in someone else's garden. I know lots of people who are doing both. If neither is an option, you can grow perennials in containers using regenerative techniques like composting and mulching. Here are a few tips to get you going.

**Find a big container.** Bigger is better when it comes to pots. Growing perennials in small pots makes it hard to take advantage of these plants' robust root structures. Rootbound or crowded plants won't weather outdoor temperature swings well and typically need more tending. A good rule of thumb is to choose a container that offers as much space below ground as a mature plant's foliage above ground.

**Keep plants well drained.** The biggest reason potted plants don't fare well over time is soggy soil. Some containers come with drainage holes, but many do not. Buy the ones that do. If your pot is over six inches wide, it needs more than one hole.

**Use potting soil.** Garden soil often becomes compacted over time. But unlike garden beds, which can be loosened with a broadfork, potted plants are almost impossible to aerate without damaging the roots. So make your own potting soil mix by combining equal parts peat moss or coconut fiber, good garden soil, compost, and sand. The peat moss and sand prevent soil from compacting and increase drainage. You can also just buy potting soil from your local garden store. Potting soil is usually mixed with perlite or vermiculite, textured styrofoam-like pebbles, to help container soil stay loose and porous. Look for potting soil that is 100 percent organic and, if you can find it, inoculated with mycorrhizae, a fungus that works with plant roots to absorb more nutrients.

**Maintain regeneratively:** While potted plants are resilient, they do take a little extra care. Garden plants have deep root structure that can find water and nutrients underground but potted plants depend on you to keep them moist and fed.

**Water:** The exposed sides of the pot absorb heat and dry out the potting soil quickly. Water your soil whenever it's dry.

**Compost:** Twice a year in the spring and fall, add valuable nutrients by layering on a half-inch of compost. I like to gently mix it into the first two inches of soil.

**Mulch:** If your potted plants live outside in the summer, cover the top of the soil with mulch to keep it from baking in the sun. Mulch also helps retain moisture, whether your plants live inside or out.

If your potted plant has stopped growing, or the roots have pushed through the drainage holes, it's time to repot. Find a new container big enough for your plant to stretch out and grow. Fill in the extra space with an equal mixture of potting soil and compost.

Yellowing leaves may mean a plant needs more nitrogen. I rely on liquid fish emulsion to quickly boost plant growth. It's simple to add, since you don't need to mix it into the soil. Dilute the concentrate with water, following the instructions on the label, and slowly pour the mixture into the pot. Be aware that fish emulsion smells pretty, well, fishy, which can be a problem for indoor plants. Cut down on the stink by adding a few drops of lavender oil before pouring.

## Where can I find information on frost dates?

Just when you think it's safe to move your potted plants outdoors in the spring, *bam*, you get hit by an overnight frost that blankets your tender plants in ice.

Predicting the last frost can be tricky, especially with climate change as a variable. I rely on freeze/frost guides maintained by the National Weather Service and Farmer's Almanac. Both organizations draw on years of record keeping by the National Center for Environmental Information (NCEI). The NCEI determines the last frost date by calculating the latest day each spring a frost has been observed 90 percent of the time.

*A row cover is a lightweight cloth that protects plants from cold, strong winds, and pesky bugs while letting in water and sunlight. Buy a cover online, or make one yourself.*

Since there's at least a 10 percent chance of an error, it's not a bad idea to monitor the weather. Bring your tender plants inside even if there's only a small chance of a late frost—why take the risk. If they're already in the ground, protect against surprise frosts by covering them with a blanket, lightweight garden fabric, or floating row cover.

## How do I make my own compost?

It's easier than it looks! Plus, you'll have the immense satisfaction of converting food scraps that might otherwise rot in a landfill and emit potent greenhouse gases, such as methane, carbon dioxide, and nitrous oxide. I still remember the first time I turned the old vegetables, coffee grounds, and newspapers I'd saved up over the summer into clean, rich, good-smelling earth. It was thrilling.

The first step to composting is to choose your composter. I like building a pile outdoors. But maybe you don't want to run the risk of attracting pests, like mice and rats. Or you don't have a big yard, or any yard at all. No matter—you can compost in closed bins or yard waste bags. Bins can be moved around and bags tucked in a corner of a porch, balcony, or garage. Many containers are divided into at least two sections so you can fill one side with fresh food waste while the other side "cures," or decomposes. But tumblers and garbage bags work fine, too.

Next, set up a system for collecting the raw material. I keep a covered bowl in my kitchen to collect food scraps like vegetable ends, egg shells, fruit rinds, and coffee grounds. You'll also want to compost cardboard, old newspaper, straw, grass clippings, and dried leaves. You can compost wood chips, but be aware that these take longer to break down.

Avoid composting bones or oily materials. Keep out meat, dairy products, fish, or peanut butter; your home compost pile won't get hot enough to render these safe. Never compost diseased plant clippings or weeds that have gone to seed or you'll spread them throughout your garden.

| Material | Brown/Green | Notes |
|----------|-------------|-------|
| Bark mulch | Brown | Bark breaks down more easily than wood chips. It's often available at low cost from a local tree service. |
| Dried plant waste | Brown | Dead or overwintered plant stalks, crops that have gone to seed, and dried leaves and stems are all a good source of brown compost. |
| Household paper | Brown | Paper towels, napkins, brown paper bags—all fair game. You can even compost junk mail as long as you shred it. |
| Leaves | Brown | Collect leaves from your local public works department for free, if you don't have enough of your own. Shred them before composting so they don't mat. |
| Newspaper/ Cardboard | Brown | Separate corrugated cardboard layers and tear into small pieces or shred what you can so it breaks down more easily. |
| Straw/Hay | Brown | Straw generally has fewer weed seeds than hay, which makes it a better choice. To be safe, buy certified weed-free material. |
| Wood chips | Brown | Wood chips are high in carbon so toss in only a few, and mix in some green stuff to help neutralize them. |
| Woody branches | Brown | Chop branches into smaller pieces so they break down more easily, or ask for shredded branches from a local tree service. |

*To build healthy compost, aim for a mix of two parts green to one part brown material. Be prepared to adjust as needed. If it's not decomposing quickly, add more of the green stuff. If it's slimy or smells bad, add more of the brown.*

| Material | Brown/Green | Notes |
|----------|-------------|-------|
| Chicken manure | Green | Chicken manure is high in nitrogen. Add it to plants in small quantities only, and be sure to spread it evenly. |
| Coffee grounds/ Tea leaves | Green | You can compost the grounds, the filters, and the tea bags. All of it. |
| Composted cow/ horse/sheep/goat manure | Green | Manure amps up compost by adding beneficial bacteria. It's easy to find at gardening stores and a little goes a long way. |
| Food scraps | Green | Collect compostable food scraps in a covered bin under the sink or on the counter. (See "What to avoid.") |
| Garden waste | Green | Yellowing leaves, trimmings, and post-harvest plants are great sources of nutrients. Sort out any diseased plants. |
| Garden weeds | Green | Weeds are okay, unless they've gone to seed. To be safe, remove seed heads before adding any to your pile. |
| Grass clippings | Green | Add in thin layers to avoid clumping. Don't use if treated with herbicide. |
| Seaweed and kelp | Green | Soil needs certain vital trace nutrients and seaweed is a great source. |
| Egg shells | Neutral | A great source of calcium. To get the most out of them, crush before adding. |
| Greenhouse waste | Neutral | Tossing together potting soil and greenhouse debris is another good way to build soil. |
| Things to avoid | "Compostable" packaging and flatware, which need intense heat to break down. Bones, pet waste, human and pet hair, glossy coated paper, fish and meat scraps, large branches, synthetic fertilizer, weeds gone to seed. | |

Good compost is made up of carbon-rich brown materials and nitrogen-rich green materials. It's this mixture that activates hard-working soil microbes. If you have a compost bin or pile, start with a layer of brown materials like leaves, straw, and wood ash, followed by a layer of green materials like grass, garden clippings, weeds, and food scraps. Aim for two parts green to one part brown, but don't worry about being precise. Fine-tuning the mix is part of the job. If your pile isn't heating up, add more green material. If it's slimy and slick, add more brown.

Since woody materials are slow to decompose, use pruners or shears to chop up any cuttings larger than a half-inch in diameter. Also, shred debris that easily mats together, like leaves and newspaper. Any clumps keep water and air from reaching the center of your pile. If I notice my compost is cold or slimy, I turn it over, usually with a pitchfork, to aerate and help break down the ingredients.

You'll know your combination is working when the pile heats up. Warmth is a sign the microbes are dining on your waste. Ideally, your compost pile will be in the range of 110–150 degrees. The bigger the pile, the warmer it will remain throughout cold winters. The warmth protects the worms and soil organisms that convert your scraps into black garden gold.

Turning waste into compost can take anywhere from four or five weeks with a tumbler to a full season with a big pile. Basically, compost is ready when it's a dark brown color and has an earthy smell. No need to wait until your compost is finished before using it. Add it to your soil at any time.

## How do I shop for compost?

Not everyone has a yard full of crumbly dead leaves, like me. Or maybe you need compost before your own home-brewed batch is ready. No problem. It's easy to pick up a bag of ready-made stuff from your local yard store.

Look for the Organic Materials Review Institute (OMRI) certification. OMRI is an international nonprofit that decides which products meet their standards for organic. You'll want to make sure the bagged compost isn't wet or slimy. When compost sits in a sealed bag in the baking sun, it can go bad or become anaerobic. So buy a sample bag to take home. If it looks dark brown, feels moist but not soggy, and has a loose or granular texture, go ahead and buy more bags.

## What can I use for mulch?

Spreading mulch is one of my favorite farm chores. I love the moment my pitchfork pierces the heaping mound of leftover grass and leaves and the steam spirals up into the cool morning air. I love the lingering scent of cedar after a day spent spreading wood chips. I also like the satisfying look of a tidy, weed-free field after I've laid down a sea of straw.

Mulch is typically used to help prevent weed growth. It also conserves moisture and insulates and protects your plants from sun, wind, cold, and erosion. Typically, it's added on top of compost in the spring, in part to help keep the compost from washing away, and in the fall to protect your plants over the winter.

For mulch, I use only organic materials that can be broken down by soil microbes. I shy away from synthetic mulches like landscape fabric because they do nothing for soil health. The best organic mulches are readily available, cheap, and easy to spread—just like my favorite all-purpose mulch.

Straw or hay, or shredded dry leaves, or some combination, is my go-to mulch. Hay is grass, like timothy, generally grown to feed livestock, and it enriches the soil as it breaks down. Straw, which is the stalk of a grain after the seeds have been removed, doesn't do much for the soil as it decomposes. But it's much less likely than hay to be full of weed seeds. If you decide to give hay a try, do your research to find the high-quality sources least likely to spread weeds.

To use either one, simply grab a bale, rip it apart, and spread it over the soil. Or mix the stalks with leaves that have been shredded by a mower or left out to dry and crumble. Don't use whole leaves, which easily mat, making it hard for water to percolate into the soil.

To keep my paths free of weeds, I use cardboard with a thin covering of more attractive looking wood chips. Most inks are soy based and safe, though I avoid using glossy boxes just to be safe. Rip your cardboard into smaller pieces or leave it whole. If you're covering a large area, make sure your cardboard pieces overlap or weeds will pop up in between them.

A thin covering of grass clippings can add nutrients, particularly phosphorus, to soil. But grass clumps thicker than one inch can get hot enough to kill your plants. Also, avoid using clippings from exceptionally weedy lawns or from areas treated with non-organic sprays.

Many gardeners use wood chips or bark. The advantage is that these materials decompose slowly, so you don't have to replace your mulch as often. But when soil microbes eat woody mulch, they use the nitrogen in the soil to break down the materials, actually depleting this nutrient around your plants. I offset this by mixing in a high-nitrogen fertilizer, such as blood meal or fish meal.

Another option is to limit the use of bark to pathways and other areas that see a lot of foot traffic. Sawdust, another woody mulch, can be messy, but acid-loving perennials like blueberries love it.

## When and how do I fertilize my plants?

Part of what makes perennials so great is that they're low maintenance and don't need much, if any, fertilizer beyond a yearly serving of compost. In fact, if you've taken steps to build healthy soil, you'll have plenty of nutrients for your perennials without having to do much more. Still, fertilizers do boost growth and can be an efficient way to treat nutritional deficiencies.

You can add whatever fertilizer you choose in one of three ways: either mix it into the first three inches of your soil along with compost before planting, add it to your existing plants in early spring, or work it into the soil of plants that need a boost during the growing season. So much energy goes into making flowers and fruit that plants can get stressed, and stressed plants attract pests. Signs of stress include wilting, dropped blossoms, and leaves that change color around the edge. Giving your flowering perennials some extra phosphorus can help keep them healthy.

Avoid adding nutrients just before a rainy period sets in because they'll just wash away. Excess nutrients enter waterways and promote harmful algae blooms that suck oxygen out of the water and kill aquatic life. If you decide to fertilize in the fall, before your plants hunker down for the winter, ditch the nitrogen and phosphorus in favor of potassium, which will help the roots.

Good all-purpose fertilizers include homemade compost, mycorrhizal inoculant (0-0-0), fish emulsion (5-2-2), and a balanced blend (10-10-10). To accelerate spring growth, try manure compost, blood meal (13-0-0), or alfalfa meal (3-1-2). To maximize fruit production you might consider bone meal (3-15-0) or guano (12-12-2.5). And to help plants fend off pests and climate stress, consider kelp meal (1-0-2), greensand (0-0-3), or organic mulch.

## What do the three numbers on store-bought fertilizer mean?

You will see a series of numbers on fertilizer bags like 10-10-10 or 20-0-5. These numbers represent the ratio of nitrogen (N), phosphorus (P), and potassium (K) in the fertilizer. The higher the number, the more concentrated the nutrient. So a mixture of 20-0-5 has four times more nitrogen than potassium and zero phosphorus.

To understand how commercial fertilizers act on plants, I like to use the phrase "up, down, and all around."

**Up:** The first number refers to the amount of available nitrogen, or the "up" factor. If you want to quickly add lush growth above ground, go for a fertilizer that is nitrogen heavy. Be careful not to add too much or you could have vigorous growth at the expense of below-ground root development. One season I used too much alfalfa meal in my homemade fertilizer blend. My potatoes took off, flashing prolific green growth that had me dreaming of a bumper crop. But when I took my pitchfork to my potatoes in late August, I discovered only a cluster of tiny nubs attached to the base of the plants.

**Down:** The middle number references the amount of phosphorus. Use more phosphorus to maximize flower and fruit production, whether you want nice rose blooms or tasty tomatoes. To encourage my fruits and veggies to ripen faster, I switch from a nitrogen-rich fertilizer to a high-phosphorus fertilizer, like bone meal, once the first flowers appear.

**All around:** The last number indicates the amount of potassium. Add a potassium-rich fertilizer to help your plants fight disease, pests, and stress from cold, heat, and wind. I always use a potassium-rich fertilizer like greensand when I tuck in my plants for the winter to help them survive the cold.

## How do I fight weeds without using herbicides?

It's easy to romanticize growing food until you've spent a backbreaking afternoon clearing your garden of weeds, only to see them sprout again a week later. But with a few quick tips, you can minimize weeding and build healthy soil at the same time.

Before you head out with hoe in hand, know what you're up against. Some weeds are shallow-rooted annuals like chickweed and miner's lettuce, while others are deep-rooted perennials like thistle and runner grass. If you're not sure what to weed out of the garden, buy a field guide to weeds.

Annual weeds are easy to remove if you wait for a hot, dry day. Use a small-toothed rake, hoe, or hand weeder. Cut off weeds just below the surface of the soil, then let them bake in the sun. For weeds taller than eight inches, you'll have to pull them out by hand.

Perennial weeds have an extensive root system that stores energy and makes them much more stubborn than annual weeds. If you don't pull out the whole root, they quickly grow back. In dry conditions, it's nearly impossible to remove the entire root, so before attacking them I always wait for a good rainstorm to soak the earth and loosen their grip. I also recommend using a weeding fork.

Another thing to keep in mind is that you want to disturb the soil as little as possible. Weed seeds can survive in the soil for many years. When you disturb the soil, you bring dormant seeds to the surface, where they sprout. The best way to keep troublesome seeds asleep is to leave your soil alone as much as possible. To rout out annuals, I use a stirrup hoe to cut weed roots an inch below the surface without turning the soil. This way, I don't wake dormant seeds.

It's worth noting that even when you try not to, you will disturb the soil. This is especially true if you're clearing a new area for planting. Honestly, the only way to get rid of weeds in your first year or two of planting is to keep at it. I weed new areas at least twice a week at dusk. That way, I avoid the hot weather and maybe get to enjoy a sunset, which distracts me somewhat from my grueling task. Also, if you weed aggressively enough the first year, new seeds are much less likely to take root. Here are a few other tips for dealing with this ongoing gardening challenge.

**Grow out your weeds.** One effective way to find and get rid of your weed seeds is to grow them out. To make this work, I prepare the soil by mixing in compost and watering. But instead of sowing vegetable seeds, I let the soil sit for a week. Once the bed is covered with little weed sprouts, I hit them with a hoe during the heat of the day so they shrivel and die. I've also been known to blast weeds with a flame torch. Whatever it takes.

**Cut off their heads.** When you don't have time to pull out weeds, walk around with a good pair of pruners or a weed wacker and chop off the flowers before they start producing seeds. I do this during the thick of summer when I have chores that take priority over weeding.

It's not as effective as pulling out weeds by their roots, but it can buy you a few weeks before ever-resilient weeds start flowering again.

**Water only the plants you want.** Create mini droughts in your garden to control your weed population. I use drip irrigation and soaker hoses to water the base of my vegetables and perennials, skipping the spaces between my plants where the weeds live.

**Smother them with mulch.** Mulch is a champion at blocking weed growth, so every spring, I spread two to four inches of it on my garden beds. For really overgrown areas, I lay down damp cardboard before covering it with a mix of dried leaves and clean hay or straw. This is usually enough to knock out even the gnarliest weeds.

**Crowd them out with a cover crop.** A traditional cover crop is a mixture of rye, clover, and vetch. But I find it hard to control these plants in a small garden setting. Instead I plant edible crops, like fast-growing lettuce or strawberries, in between and around my plants. The result is more food and fewer weeds.

## What organic pest solutions can I use?

Organic gardeners shy away from using pesticides for some very good reasons. Sprays can kill beneficial bugs, like the bees that pollinate your raspberries or the insects that cycle nutrients through your soil. Pesticides also find their way into the food chain because plants absorb the chemicals through their roots and leaves. You can mitigate the risk by relying on the following pesticides, which have been certified for organic use by the nonprofit OMRI.

**Note:** Certified organic or not, pesticides should be kept in their original containers out of the reach of pets and children. Store them in a dark, dry place in temperatures between 40 and 100 degrees. I keep mine in a closet in my house rather than in my uninsulated garden shed.

**NEEM OIL:** This oil comes from the bark and leaves of the neem tree, a common evergreen grown in tropical and subtropical regions. Azadirachtin, the active ingredient, makes insects grow more slowly and eat less. It also makes them lose interest in laying eggs. Neem is particularly effective against fast-growing beetles, small caterpillars, and aphids.

Use neem on plants as soon as you see an adult bug and spray weekly. Keep your bees safe by covering treated plants with a row cover. Don't expect neem to instantly rid your garden of pests. It works over time by limiting the reproduction and growth of pests. If you want to speed up the process, hand-pluck adult bugs from your plants.

**INSECTICIDAL SOAP:** Insecticidal soaps are an effective way to control soft-bodied insects when no beneficial bugs are around to do the job for you. The fatty acids in insecticidal soaps break down the protective cuticles of soft-bodied pests like aphids and caterpillars, which become dehydrated and die.

Soap sprays only kill insects that are sprayed directly, so be sure to thoroughly wet both sides of the leaves. Avoid spraying beneficial insects like bees and spiders. Repeat applications every five to seven days as new pests hatch and form colonies.

**How to prepare it:** Make your own soap spray by adding one tablespoon of dishwashing soap for every quart of water. Or buy an insecticidal soap concentrate and follow the instructions. Mix only as much concentrate as you need for the day and keep spray bottles out of the sun. Dilute any unused sprays with more water and pour it outside, far away from storm drains.

**DIATOMACEOUS EARTH (DE):** DE is made from the pulverized fossils of tiny sea creatures. If you peer at it under a microscope, it looks like broken glass. This white powder kills insects by slicing up their protective outer layer. Dust the leaves of your plants to kill leaf-eating bugs, like newly hatched Japanese beetles and wireworms. Or create a barrier of white powder at the base of your plants to stop slugs. It works best in dry conditions because rain makes the powder congeal in clumps and lose some of its sharp edges. If it rains, reapply DE after your plants have dried.

**BACILLUS THURINGIENSIS (Bt):** *Bacillus thuringiensis*, or Bt, is a naturally occurring bacteria that ruptures the guts of leaf-eating insects like caterpillars. It only works on bugs that eat the treated leaves. It has no impact on pests that are directly sprayed, so bees and other pollinators are safe. Direct sunlight degrades Bt after a few hours, so apply it late in the day when the sun is low and pests are about to begin their nightly feeding. You can use Bt every 10 days.

**SPINOSAD:** Spinosad is made from a naturally occurring bacteria, *Saccharopolyspora spinosa*, which produces a deadly neurotoxin that makes infected insects excited to the point of utter exhaustion. After eating the bacteria, insects immediately stop feeding and die within a few days. Spinosad works to control all types of caterpillars and some beetles that eat a lot of leaf tissue.

Apply spinosad to dry leaves as soon as you notice leaf-eating pests in your garden. Thoroughly wet both sides of the leaves. Spinosad breaks down in direct sun, so late afternoon applications are the most effective. Spinosad is absorbed by plant leaves, and one treatment can last up to 10 days. Within the first 24 hours of spraying, be careful not to let treated leaves come in contact with beneficial insects like bees. Protect your good bugs by draping treated plants in row covers for the first day.

**PLANTSKYDD®:** I know people who swear by this environmentally safe pest repellent. It works for up to six months—even over the winter—against rabbits, voles, moose, chipmunks, squirrels, nutria, beaver, groundhogs, and deer. This chemical emits an odor that smells like the pests' predators, scaring unwelcome visitors away from your garden.

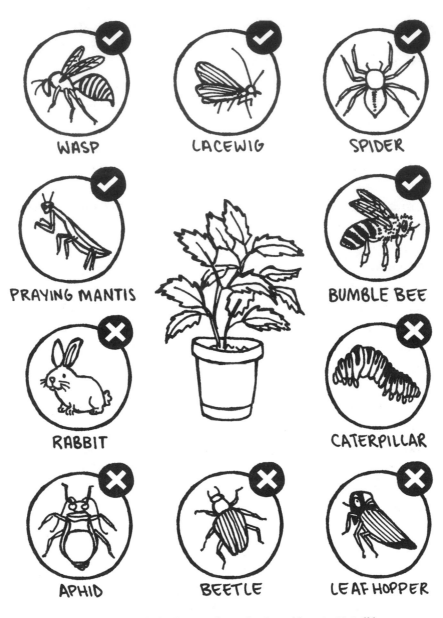

WASP

LACEWIG

SPIDER

PRAYING MANTIS

BUMBLE BEE

RABBIT

CATERPILLAR

APHID

BEETLE

LEAF HOPPER

*Common garden pests include plant-eating animals and insects. Not all bugs are bad. Honeybees pollinate your crops and lacewings devour aphids. Spiders are also a gardener's best friend. The world's spider population eats up to 800 million tons of insects each year.*

# How do I grow tomatoes and peppers year round?

Tomatoes and peppers are examples of tender perennials, plants that cannot survive a light frost and must be brought inside during the winter. Bringing them indoors lets me eat fresh tomatoes and peppers in February. Other examples include basil, New Zealand spinach, and sweet potatoes.

Indirect winter sun is often too weak to do the job of keeping them alive, so use a grow light, which mimics direct sunlight and adds warmth. Without a grow light, you'll need to crank up your thermostat for most of each day. Water your indoor plants when the first two inches of soil are dry.

Here are four easy techniques for keeping your tender perennials alive through the winter.

**Grow them in pots.** Grow your tender perennials in pots all year round so when it starts getting cold, you can just move them indoors. This works well for compact peppers and tomatoes. For larger perennials, like vining cherry tomatoes, let the fruit ripen, harvest your fruit, cut the branches about two inches from the soil, and then move the plants indoors.

Before moving any plants inside, make sure they're free of bugs and disease. If you keep your tender perennials in a pot all year, fertilize them with a 10-10-10 fertilizer to keep them happy since they won't be able to draw any nutrients from your outdoor garden soil.

**Dig them up.** You can grow your tender perennials outdoors during the summer and move them into pots in the fall. When transplanting, don't just grab hold of a plant and yank it out of the ground. Instead, take a perennial shovel and gently loosen the soil around the plant, being careful of the roots. Once the plant is free, put it in a pot with enough room for the roots. The shock of being pulled out of the ground is bad enough for a plant without also having to adjust to a cramped new home. Make sure your pot contains a mix of compost and soil.

Before bringing them inside, water your repotted plants. Give them enough that water drains through the bottom of the pot. Pruning your plants to half their height can also help them survive the transition.

**Use cuttings.** Some perennials are too big to repot. For these plants, take cuttings and let them take root inside. To create a cutting, snip off a plant shoot and stick it in a pot full of soil and compost. Water it and move to a sunny windowsill or set it under a grow light.

**Force them into a dormant state.** If you don't have the space or light to keep your perennials happy in the winter, cut them back to six to eight inches from the base of the plant. Keep them in a cool but not cold place; around 50 degrees works well for the winter. Water them once a month. Dormant plants need no sunlight and require little water. As spring approaches, move your plants to a warmer, well-lit area to wake them up. Then watch them grow. Your plants will be hardier and produce food much more quickly than new sprouts will.

## What's the best way to move plants from a pot into the ground?

Indoor plants often have a hard time adjusting to an outdoor location. After all, they've lived coddled lives in the warmth and protection of your home. So it's worth doing whatever you can to ease the stress of transplanting.

One strategy for avoiding transplant shock is to use biodegradable pots. All you have to do is create a hole for the pots. Nature does the rest of the work. The pots, often made of peat or manure, add nutrients to the soil as they decompose, and keep plastic out of landfills.

You'll need to acclimate your seedlings gradually to the outdoors no matter what pots you use. One week before transplanting your sprouts, move your potted plants outside so they can feel the breeze and sun. At night, if temperatures are still cold, move them back inside.

On moving day, dig holes about twice as big as the pots and add compost. Lower in your biodegradable pots, and fill in the holes. If you have plastic pots, gently free your plants from their containers by running a knife around the edge. You want to keep as much soil as possible attached to the roots. Be careful not to plant your seedlings too deep; if the stem is covered with soil, it might rot.

Always water newly transplanted seedlings to reduce stress and firm up the soil. I prefer transplanting seedlings during a light rain or on a cloudy day to avoid shocking the plants with direct sunlight.

*Choosing the right container can help get your plants off to a strong start. I like biodegradable pots because they allow you to skip the transplantation process, while adding nutrients to the soil as they decompose. Small clustered pots or cells work nicely if you're starting small seeds like herbs. They also stack neatly on a heat mat. I favor larger, two-inch pots, because they're so versatile. For root cuttings, stick them in a one-gallon pot before transplanting them.*

# Glossary

**Bare root:** Bare root plants are grown directly in the ground before being sold. Growing plants in the ground instead of in a container promotes healthy, spreading roots. It's best to dig up and transplant bare root plants in early spring, when they're likely to be dormant.

**Bloom:** The waxy or powdery coating found on the surface of some fruits, like blueberries and grapes. It prevents fruit from rotting or drying out and becoming wrinkly. If you plan on storing berries or fruit, avoid washing off the bloom so they last longer.

**Bolting:** Premature flowering due to changes in temperature or length of the day, stress, or thirst. Plants bolt to produce seeds quickly before they die.

**Cane:** The flexible woody stem of plant like a raspberry or blackberry. Unlike a branch, a cane comes out of the ground. A raspberry bush consists of a lot of canes shooting out of the soil independently.

**Carbon sink:** A natural reservoir that absorbs carbon from the atmosphere and stores it. Plants, soil, and oceans are carbon sinks.

**Companion plant:** Since plants have natural friends and foes in the garden, maximizing these relationships helps create a resilient space. Certain combinations of plants work to control pests, enhance growth, increase flavor, and create habitat for the good bugs you want to keep around. Plants also have foes that deter growth and stunt productivity.

**Cover crop:** Any plant grown for the benefit of the soil rather than for harvest. Cover crops are used to suppress weeds, prevent erosion, improve soil fertility, and control disease and pests. Cover crops are typically grasses or low-growing groundcovers like clover, but they can also be any green plant grown for these reasons.

**Cutting:** A section of a plant taken from the stem, leaf, or root that is capable of developing into a new plant. *Taking a cutting* refers to clipping or trimming a certain part of a plant and then rooting it to create a clone of the mother plant. Plants grown from cuttings often mature more quickly than those grown from seed.

**Direct seeding:** A method of planting in which seeds are placed directly in the soil where they will grow, as opposed to first being planted in pots before being moved outside.

**Dividing:** A technique for controlling the size of your perennials. Once plants are established and thriving, they may get crowded. Dividing them rejuvenates growth and helps spread carbon-sucking perennials around the garden.

**Dormant:** The period of rest in a plant's life cycle. In general, plants become dormant in the winter to conserve energy so they can regrow the following spring. Some plants enter dormancy to protect themselves in extreme heat or drought.

**Flash freeze:** A method of preserving fruits and vegetables by spreading them in a single layer on a baking sheet and placing it in the freezer for 15 minutes. Flash freezing helps guard against freezer burn and prevents produce from freezing into a solid clump.

**Germination:** The process by which a seed begins to sprout after being planted in soil. For a seed to germinate, water, light, and temperature have to be just right. In the right conditions, the seed coat breaks apart and a root emerges from the opening, followed by a plant shoot.

**Girdle:** When a root or band wraps tightly around the trunk or stem of a plant. Water and nutrients can't flow from the base of the plant to the leaves, eventually killing the plant.

**Heavy feeders:** Plants that need more nutrients than the average plant. Examples include broccoli, asparagus, tomatoes, and peppers. Heavy feeders benefit from having nutrients added to the soil during the growing season.

**Sheet mulch:** Also known as *lasagna mulch*, sheet mulch refers to layers of cardboard, seaweed, leaves, and grass (or any combination of organic materials) laid down to kill weeds and build healthy soil.

**Legumes:** Plants from the pea family including beans, peas, and clover. Legumes have nodules on their roots that contain nitrogen-fixing bacteria. The bacteria work with the plant roots to take nitrogen from the air and add it to the soil.

**Mycelium:** The vegetative part of mushrooms and fungus made of thin white threads called *hyphae*. Masses of hyphae make up a network of mycelium that interacts with plant roots, exchanging nutrients for carbon-rich sugars. This relationship is very important as it extends the surface area of plant roots so they get more out of the soil. This dramatically increases plant resilience.

**OMRI:** The Organic Materials Review Institute is an international nonprofit that labels those products permitted for organic production. The organization has strict guidelines and carefully researches each product before giving it the seal of approval.

**Pore space:** The volume of space between soil particles that can be filled with water or air. Sandy soil has large pore space and can absorb a lot of water, then drain quickly. Clay soil has small pore space and absorbs less water, then drains slowly. The ideal soil, or loamy soil, has both large and small pore spaces that provide good drainage while maintaining good soil moisture.

**Propagation:** The process of creating new plants from seeds or cuttings.

**Prune:** The process of cutting off dead, overgrown, or diseased branches, stems, or buds. Regular pruning stimulates plant growth so that you have healthier plants and abundant harvests. Most plants benefit from regular pruning.

**Root crown:** The transition point from the plant's roots to the aboveground growth of a plant at the stem. Certain plants, like asparagus, grow from root crowns.

**Rooting hormone:** A combination of naturally occurring plant growth hormones that promote root growth. The hormone stimulates growth by helping cuttings switch from producing green or vegetative cells to growing root cells. Rooting hormone comes in powder, gel, and liquid form. Most plant cuttings naturally produce their own rooting hormones, but synthetic rooting hormone helps produce higher-quality roots quicker so your perennials grow faster.

**Scarification:** Some seeds have a hard seed coat to survive the winter before they sprout. This defense can slow or even prevent germination. Scratching the seed before you plant helps water move past the protective seed coat so it can sprout. Seeds are naturally scarified by cycles of freeze/thaw, or by critters that nibble at the seeds. A gardener can mimic this process by scraping seeds with a knife or scratching them gently with sandpaper.

**Self-sowing:** Occurs when seeds mature, or completely dry out, and fall to the ground, where they germinate the next growing season. Also called *volunteering*.

**Soil compaction:** The loss of air pockets between the tiny particles that make up the structure of soil, making it harder for roots to push through. Heavy machinery or foot traffic can cause this. Compacted soil is associated with poor plant growth and lack of resilience.

**Soil structure:** A soil's particular arrangement of particles and pore space. This can be friable or dense, depending on how soil particles clump together or aggregate. Sandy soils have a loose structure, while clay soils are much more dense. Adding compost to any type of soil will improve its structure and promote water and air movement as well as increase biological activity, root growth, and seed germination.

**Tender perennials:** A plant that can live for more than a year but only if brought inside during the winter. Tender perennials cannot survive a light frost. Examples include tomatoes, basil, and peppers.

**Trace minerals:** Micronutrients essential to plant growth. Unlike nitrogen, potassium, and phosphorus, which are needed in large quantities, trace elements like boron, copper, manganese, and zinc are needed in very small amounts. Without them, plants cannot flourish.

**Vernalization:** The exposure of plants or seeds to cold temperatures to stimulate flowers or germination. This cold treatment, also known as cold stratification, can promote growth. The process is important if you're growing cold weather crops in a warm climate.

# Acknowledgments

I have been living and breathing this book for more than a year now. It is what I worked on before leaving the house every day. It is what I came home to every night. Early on I learned to carry around a notebook so I could jot down thoughts mid-weeding, or mulching, or planting. It was never far from my mind, which was fine by me. The chance to write a book about growing food in hopes of inspiring others to do the same has been an adventure, and a privilege.

This book is not mine alone. It has been a team effort from the start. Our mighty researchers include Nancy Chang and Lauren Chan, who dug deep to help pull together many of our perennial profiles. Lydia Chodosh lent her design expertise to making them useful and easy to read. Sophic Nau spent long hours in her kitchen giving shape and structure to the sometimes haphazard way I cook with these foods. Ryan Scheife, our layout designer, patiently rolled with it when the book doubled in size from the beginning to the end of the project.

Illustrator Krishna Chavda brought to life these wonderful foods through her attention to detail and beautifully rendered drawings. Thank you for your patience and commitment to making every one of them just right as we went through the laborious process of figuring out what to include, and what to leave out. Another big thanks goes to Gregory Veitch, a writer and regenerative farmer who pored over the book six times! His tough questions, insightful comments, and diligent research did a lot to strengthen the book.

Our editorial team bulged with capable souls. It included Elisse Gabriel, Paula Fleming, and the tireless Virginia Aronson, who cheerfully read the entire manuscript more times than I can count, and nonetheless continued to find ways to improve on it. I could not be more grateful for my editor and publisher, Clare Ellis, who shared in many laughs and sleepless nights as we ushered this book through to completion. Thank you for believing in me and pushing me to become what I've always wanted to be. Your guidance has been indispensable.

To my friends and family who put up with me during this process. I know the countless, "I'm sorry I can't do that right now, I'm writing a book," got old. And to my steady companion Nimbus, I promise to take you for more walks in the woods now that the book is done.

**Acadia Tucker** has a life-long love affair with plants that has led her around the world, mapping endemic plant species on the Channel Islands and conducting plant surveys deep in the Peruvian rainforest. After graduating from Pitzer College, she started a four-season organic market garden in Washington State inspired by farming pioneers Eliot Coleman and Jean-Martin Fortier. While managing the farm, Acadia grew 200 different food crops before heading back to school at the University of British Columbia to complete a Masters in Land and Water Systems. She lives in New Hampshire with her farm dog, Nimbus, and grows hops to support locally sourced craft beer in New England, when she isn't raising perennials in her own backyard. Acadia is also the author of *Growing Good Food: A citizen's guide to backyard carbon farming* (Stone Pier Press).

**Krishna Chavda** is an illustrator, educator, and pattern designer. She earned her MFA in Illustration from Savannah College of Art and Design and now creates artwork for books, apparel, and magazines. Krishna currently lives in Hoboken, New Jersey with her 16 plants, and has a stationery line featuring her illustrations under the name NANU Studio.